LADY LIBERTY'S TREASURE HUNT

Best friends forever (photograph by Laurel Burke O'Connell)

LADY LIBERTY'S
TREASURE HUNT

A Memoir, and Adventure

MICHAEL CLOHERTY O'CONNELL

Two Lanterns illustration by Monica Vachula Paul Revere's Ride 2003

Hardcover ISBN: 979-8-9918207-0-7
Paperback ISBN: 979-8-9918207-1-4

Published by
One Then Two Lanterns LLC
11 LaMancha Way, Andover, MA 01810
Website & Blog: ladylibertystreasurehunt.com
Email: mco@ladylibertystreasurehunt.com

"If you truly want to understand the present, or yourself, you must begin in the past. History is not simply a study of the past, it's an explanation of the present."

—Inspired by the movie, The Holdovers (2023)

The Frost Farm Derry, New Hampshire (photograph by Michael O'Connell)

INTRODUCTION

Before we begin this tale, I want to share some important wisdom, written long ago in a poem by Robert Frost. He lived on a farm at 122 Rockingham Road in Derry, New Hampshire in a home his Grandfather gave him when he married. It's now a New Hampshire State Historic Site, and beautiful park. Please enjoy those trails on his Derry Farm as I have so many times.

Robert Frost Sculpture at his Stone House Museum in Shaftsbury, Vermont (Public Domain)

"THE ROAD NOT TAKEN"
by Robert Frost:

"Two roads diverged in a yellow wood,
And sorry I could not travel both
And be one traveler, long I stood
And looked down one as far as I could
To where it bent in the undergrowth;
Then took the other, as just as fair,
And having perhaps the better claim,
Because it was grassy and wanted wear;
Though as for that, the passing there
Had worn them really about the same,
And both that morning equally lay
In leaves no step had trodden black.
Oh, I kept the first for another day!
Yet knowing how way leads on to way,
I doubted if I should ever come back.
I shall be telling this with a sigh
Somewhere ages and ages hence:
Two roads diverged in a wood, and I --
I took the one less traveled by,
And that has made all the difference."

Robert Frost Stone House Museum at Bennington College Vermont (Public Domain)

Robert Frost and his family later moved to an apple farm now called the Robert Frost Stone House Museum (at Bennington College) 121 Vermont Rte 7A Shaftsbury, Vermont is where he lived out much of his life. Robert Frost was so famous that he was selected to read at poem at President Kennedy's Inauguration in 1961.

Frost Farm side view from the Vermont Land Trust trail (photo by author)

There is a beautiful mile trail through Frost's apple orchard, red pines, and woods toward Pan Creek. It's a nice place to enjoy nature, and listen to the bird song. I spotted a Northern Cardinal on my right, then a Woodpecker, and a Blue Jay further up wooded trail. My grandmother Mary Ann (Doherty) O'Connell loved Cardinals but often called Blue Jays bullies for taking all her birdseed from smaller birds. The song "Cardinal" by Kacey Musgraves reminds me of my grandmother.

Robert Frost's poem articulates the challenges of life, frustrations, and a love of life. I believe he tries to give those who have read his works perspectives on life so they may reflect upon it and perhaps apply it to their own lives. Robert Frost's life was filled with tragedy but yet he saw the simple beauty in life. Frost chose the epithat on his gravestone from a final line in one of his poems "I Had A Lover's Quarrel With The World." He and his family are buried nearby at Old Bennington Cemetery Bennington; if you wish to pay your respects, as I did.

Robert Frost wrote this beautiful poem while he lived here at his beautiful Vermont Stone House Apple Farm.

"Sleeping by Woods on a Snowy Evening"
by Robert Frost

"Whose woods these are I think I know.
His house is in the village though;
He will not see me stopping here
To watch his woods fill up with snow.
My little horse must think it queer
To stop without a farmhouse near
Between the woods and frozen lake
The darkest evening of the year.
He gives his harness bells a shake
To ask if there is some mistake.
The only other sound's the sweep
Of easy wind and downy flake.
The woods are lovely, dark and deep,
But I have promises to keep,
And miles to go before I sleep,
And miles to go before I sleep."

This book is not unlike Robert Frost's immortal poems. It's about a 60-year-old man looking back in time. In this work, I try to pass on some small things I have learned in this epic journey we call life. I truly hope you enjoy the book and the special time with your friends and family as you search for Lady Liberty's Treasure.

I think the moment of pause reaches many people when they turn 60, and realize there are more years behind them then ahead. Those memories from the spring and summer seasons of your life become meaningful. For reasons that I can't truly explain now, this revelation came upon me within the past few years. I think it's about our mortality and the yearning to pass on anything we have learned that may help the future.

My memories quickly jumped back to when I first met my wife in 1979 at Diamond Middle School soccer fields. Laurel and her brother Dave rode up on their bicycles. We were all coaching the Fall Saturday morning youth soccer clinic.

Laurel and Dave Burke had just moved to Lexington, and both seemed very nice. Their whole family played soccer, so they knew the sport well. Dave and Laurel were not just siblings; they were also very close friends. They were so close, that I actually thought they were twins. I learned later that Laurel was a year older than her brother Dave. She also had three more brothers: Chris, Michael, and Brian. A large Irish American - French Canadian Catholic family.

The Burkes were all heavily involved in academics, sports, church, work, and other youth activities. They were a very close and beautiful family. They were all raised lovingly in Prospect Hill area by their parents, David and Barbara Burke. Their Mom grew up in Connecticut, and their Dad in Queens, New York City.

Their parents met while Mr. Burke was serving in the US Navy at Groton, Connecticut. They were such a close-knit military family because they had to rely on each other when moving a number of times to New York, Connecticut, Virginia, and Massachusetts.

The Burke Family, and I attended Saint Brigid's Parish Lexington. Their family was so large they took up a whole row at the church. My parents and siblings did not attend church often so I was always there alone.

Time flew by, and I was at Laurel's Class of '83 graduation. Then time kept going, and her brother David graduated with the Class of '84. Laurel chose Boston College and lucked out by becoming roommates with her close LHS classmate and friend, Susan Reynolds. Dave chose Providence College and joined US Army ROTC.

I was a commuter student at Northeastern University in Boston by 1984. Laurel and I were both very busy either studying or working, but we would eventually cross paths again in Lexington Center, where we both worked in the summer of 1986.

As I got to know Laurel better, I remembered singing the famous Carpenter's song "Close to You" in 6th grade at Adams School. The song was a favorite of our great teacher Mr. Bob Farias. He loved getting the students to sing contemporary early '70s songs, and we all loved him, so we did our best. After maturing, I could actually understand what the metaphors in that great song meant.

"Why do birds suddenly appear every time you are near? Just like me, they long to be close to you. Why do stars fall down from the sky every time you walk by? Just like me, they long to be close to you. On the day that you were born, the angels got together, and decided to create a dream come true. So they sprinkled moon dust in your hair and golden starlight in your eyes of blue."

I believe the angels really did create Laurel that way. She was a dream come true. "For I can't help falling in love with you" by Elvis Presley, pretty well summed up how I felt. She had amazing deep blue eyes. To me, she was like a supermodel. Smart, beautiful, fun, and amazing. We shared so many laughs, and had our whole lives ahead of us.

The small pieces of our lives form an unbroken chain of events. It's hard to understand much of it until you are approaching 60. I guess that's the wisdom my elders always tried to explain to me but it was always so hard for me to contemplate as I toiled through the daily efforts of life and learning. Laurel and I were trying to learn about life and love just like the words in Ed Sheeran's beautiful song "First Times."

I found a timeless treasure here (photograph by Dave Burke)

I was next transported back in time to the dance floor at our wedding reception in 1990 at Nashawtuc Country Club at the Concord & Sudbury, Massachusetts line. What a beautiful golf club to visit right in the center of the events of April 19, 1775. "Endless Love" by Lionel Richie and Diana Ross was playing as we started our married life together. Is there anything more beautiful than young love?

The crowd cheered, the thunder clapped, and the angels wept tears from heaven in the falling rain. Love, beautiful love, our love was endless. Laurel had my gold wedding band inscribed "My Endless Love, Laurel

8-11-90." The wedding band I gave her is inscribed: "Forever Yours, Michael 8-11-90."

Zach Bryan's song "Sun to Me" depicts how much I truly love, and respect her. "The only bad you've ever done was to see the good in me... I've seen hard times, bad luck, all that in-between. Sweetest of the sunflowers, yeah, you're the sun to me (Zach Bryan)."

I was hers, and she was mine forever. Laurel's love and innocence were like the beautiful song "Both Sides Now" sung by Emilia Jones in the famous Gloucester, Massachusetts-based movie "CODA." Our love was special and was meant to be endless. Laurel and I have always enjoyed our time in Rockport, Gloucester, Manchester by the Sea, Essex, and Marblehead over the years. The North Shore is really beautiful.

Laurel my beautiful BC girl at Castle Rock Marblehead (photograph by Michael O'Connell)

Laurel and I became close friends in Lexington in the summer of '86. "Take My Breath Away" by Berlin and "Boys of Summer" by Don Henley were playing on the radio as we drove north to the beach in Rockport, Massachusetts on our first date. We ate lunch, enjoyed the beach, and went in all the cute shops. It was an amazing day because I was with Laurel. She was just so much fun.

Laurel's gorgeous blue eyes were deep blue like the Atlantic Ocean, and her beautiful face and smile proved angels were real. I wanted to kiss her so badly but tried to be cool and not be too forward. As I held her hand, I felt like Dan Hill's great song "Sometimes When We Touch."

Laurel joked to me that I looked at every pretty girl in Rockport that day. I smiled and said, "You're right, I looked at every girl today and compared them to your beauty, and you are the most beautiful woman in Rockport." What a line, but in fact, I was being honest. She really was the most beautiful girl in Rockport that day. I was the luckiest guy in the world, and I think on that very day, I started to fall in love with Laurel.

Christina Perri's beautiful song "A Thousand Years" describes this type of love. It's meant to last forever across time. Laurel soon moved back to Boston College (BC) to start her senior year. She was 21, so beautiful, and ready to conquer the world.

Before I knew it, we were hanging out at Boston College while the radio played David Foster's beautiful "Love Theme from St. Elmo's Fire." College years are the best! I felt like John Parr's great song "Man in Motion (St. Elmo's Fire)."

Laurel and I enjoyed White Mountain Creamery ice cream with all her roommates, attended BC football games, ate dinner, and studied for hours in the BC Libraries. We had a GPA contest, loser had to buy dinner. Laurel crushed me. God bless her, the young woman was very smart.

We saw the 1986 movie "About Last Night" featuring Demi Moore and Rob Lowe. Laurel contemplated Whitney Houston's song "How Will I Know If He Really Loves Me?" It was a valid question as we slowly fell for each other and grew in our love.

Laurel loved the Genesis Phil Collins song "In Too Deep." We were sitting together in her Boston College dorm at Hillside in the spring of 1987, and she told me to listen closely to the words. "All the time I was searching with nowhere to run to, it started me thinking. Wondering what I had to make of my life, and who'd be waiting? Asking all kinds of questions to myself but never finding the answers... So listen, listen to me. Oh you must believe me. I can feel your eyes go through me but I don't why?" We were falling in love, "In Too Deep" and playing for keeps. She was my beautiful BC girl, and I knew someday she'd wear my ring.

I came back to reality in 2022, realizing that life was a journey; and as we grow older, of course, we look back at our whole lives because that is what made us what we are. Is it destiny? Is it fate? Is it chance? Is it God? Maybe "it's a little bit everything," like that great Dawes song. Perhaps Jackson Browne explains these feelings better than I do in his famous and beautiful song: "The Pretender."

Vadala Family at Steve Bartlett's North Manchester Park (photograph by Michael O'Connell)

Our dear friends Steve Bartlett and Christine Vadala Maglio (LHS '82) invited us up to River Rd Manchester, NH for a scenic hike on the beautiful trails at Stark Farm & a summer concert. What a thoughtful and beautiful couple they are. Steve is a descendant of Josiah Bartlett, a delegate to the Continental Congress, Founding Father, and signer of the Declaration of Independence! There is a monument in this park after an American Revolutionary War hero so it must have made Steve Bartlett feel at home with his ancestors being so notable.

In the shadow of a General's sword (photograph by Steve Bartlett)

The beautiful town of Bartlett, New Hampshire is named after Josiah Bartlett. My wife and family love to stay up there at the Grand Summit Club, enjoy the White Mountains, visit scenic Jackson with its gorgeous covered bridge and waterfalls, Old Covered Bridge Conway, and downtown North Conway. Laurel and I love covered bridges. We are always searching for these historic covered bridges in our travels in MA, ME, NH, VT, CT, RI, NY, NJ or PA. They are so beautiful, amazing architecture, some with record-breaking lengths, and help us to remember times long past. The "Bridges of Madison County" movie is about such beautiful old covered bridges.

Great ride on North Conway Scenic Trains (courtesy of North Conway Scenic Railroad)

I love the old train station and roundabout at the Scenic Conway Railroad in NH. I even took my friend Peter "Rock" Scopa to the historic North Conway Train Depot. I own one of their green Fleece Scenic Train coats. Do the train ride with your family and they will love it. My family normally goes to Zeb's General Store for candy, and treats while I visit my trains!!! Laurel prefers Jackson's Covered Bridge and waterfall to my scenic trains. We have been to Jackson many times. It's a great place to have a picnic and relax.

I jumped in the car in July 2023 and drove north following the mighty Merrimack River to the "Live Free or Die" state, then to River St in North Manchester. What a charming park with a beautiful white gazebo for "Another Tequila Sunrise" concert playing Eagles or Don Henley songs all afternoon. So cool to look back in time, listen to the music, and remember the past. Let's all seize the treasured moments as they come.

Christine Maglio brought her parents, George and Ann Vadala, from Lexington. They loved the concert, and the treasure of their loved ones in the park. The song's words echoed "so put me on a highway, show me a sign, and take it to the limit one more time" (Eagles). And we all sang along and clapped so loud for the band.

Our youngest son was heading off to college soon. Now it's our turn to become empty nesters. Family and friends is our great treasure! Time just doesn't stop for any of us.

Family shot some years back in the North Shore fog (photograph by Chris Burke)

So I guess, I started thinking that I want to name a treasure hunt after my beautiful bride of 30-plus years. I also wanted to tell our story a bit, and how life led me to her. I mention previous girlfriends not out of regret but because the lessons they taught me helped lead me to Laurel. Without them, I would never have found Laurel or she me. Our life is a journey, and everyone in our lives is part of that story.

I think everyone's life is an important tale and a lesson to others. We should all try to leave a little of what we learned behind on this journey of life for future generations. Maybe there is wisdom in this idea, or perhaps not, but this is a worthy endeavor just the same. Perhaps I could find time to write a memoir?

I try to respect and honor others that have come and gone before us, particularly those that positively impacted our nation's history in the Northeast US states. "Because it's the world I know" (Collective Soul). This book is an attempt to achieve all these purposes.

I willfully use a great many music references in this work to help put the reader in the time, place, or feeling of the moments I am describing, and because I simply love music. So if I were seeking treasure and reading this book, I would use a smartphone, and listen to each song I mention in this work. Please support all these musicians and their labels. Their music encourages us and makes each day special. As I'm typing this, "Comfortably Numb" by Pink Floyd is quietly playing in the background inspiring me.

At a minimum, you will have a good road trip listening to many songs that I have enjoyed throughout my life, even if our musical tastes differ. Perhaps start with "Boston" by Augustana because many of you live far away, and may need to plan ahead for a vacation week there. Obviously, multiple states are all in play, so this adult treasure hunt is harder than my other book, *Riley's Treasure Chase* for young adults, which is only in Massachusetts.

Famous authors & dear friends Forrest Fenn, and Doug Preston (courtesy of Doug Preston)

As an ode to Forrest Burke Fenn and his immortal The Thrill of the Chase let's get out there, enjoy the sunshine, and get some exercise and fresh air. I consider Forrest Fenn to be a Western icon and USAF military hero. With respect to Forrest, here is a tribute song in his memory: "Hero" by Family of the Year.

We are so fortunate to live in the United States of America. We are only temporary visitors on these lands. So who owns what does not concern these great treasures of natural beauty, nor does it concern Lady Liberty's Treasure Hunt or Chase. Those who possess the spirit of a pirate are not bound by others' rules. Pirates view all lands as their own as they try to make their mark on this world.

Mother Earth and posterity truly own the lands of our beautiful Northeast states and great nation. Please be respectful to her, clean up your trash, recycle, and reduce our carbon footprint on this planet. Try to help future generations, hundreds of years after we have long passed, to enjoy this beautiful place we call Earth.

Please go on this fun journey with me across time, like the truly great Styx song "Come Sail Away" with a pirate's spirit of adventure. The quest for the holy grail of my treasure is now yours to enjoy. Ride off now like a brave and wise Blue Knight on your journey of discovery.

I deliberately bounce back and forth through time in this book because all of the contents are memories. Much or none of it is in proper chronological order. Why? Because that is not how our mind stores memories. They are more like layers of thoughts intermixed over time, blowing together on autumn's winds like colorful maple leaves. As I close in on age 61, I realize winter is coming for all of us. That is why we must make the most of all the seasons of our lives.

Unfortunately, I do not that many pictures of my childhood to display in this work. A sibling of mine took them all after our parents passed. Sadly, they were likely lost to time so long ago. Too bad, I would like to have shared a few more photographs with all of you. Fortunately, my God Mother and Aunt Marion (O'Connell)

Dolan had taken some photographs of me as a youth. She meant the world to me. She was a wise old Owl, and always tried to pass on life lessons, and treasured family memories.

Regarding the missing family photographs, my older brother Joe said: "Folks do what they do, don't worry about it, and keep being you." We all must just move forward on the monopoly board of time and place. The game of life is not always fair. Just try to do your best with the hand you are dealt in life.

This situation reminds me of the words in the two famous Boston songs "Foreplay/Long Time" and "Don't Look Back." The 70s and early 80s were just amazing to me. I had so many friends from Lexington High and Lexington Minuteman Vocational School, especially in the classes of 1978 through 1986. They were the best! We cranked up "Dream On" by Aerosmith. We were all so full of hope and promise.

All of my friends' student yearbook pictures are permanently housed at the Cary Memorial Library Lexington Special Collections. There are lots of good research materials there. My wife and I spent hundreds of hours in that great library studying for our high school diplomas and college degrees.

Laurel achieved much at Lexington High School & Boston College and became a "Double Eagle." I have always been proud of my BC girl. I used to bring her Jolly Ranchers candy to keep her sharp as she studied hard all those years. She would quite literally stay until the library closed each night while she was studying for her undergraduate program and then her law degree. Smart, nice, kind and beautiful. Laurel is truly amazing. Like an angel sent down from heaven or a Saint walking among us mortals.

When Laurel hears me refer to her as an angel or Saint; she will some times correct me, and say I'd really rather be known as the mother of my four children. That's a really beautiful thing. My children are indeed fortunate to have such a loving mother.

Perhaps treasure searchers should consider buying a bag of red licorice, some Sour Patch candies, and a bag of Jolly Ranchers as I did for my road trips all over Maine, New Hampshire, Vermont, Massachusetts, Connecticut, Rhode Island, New York, New Jersey, and Pennsylvania to hide Lady Liberty's treasure. But where, and how many treasures are out there? That's up to you great searchers, your children, and perhaps their children to figure out. God knows how long it will take? Remember all 9 states are in play!!!!!!!!!

When I was dating Laurel, I always felt like the immortal words in Bruce Springsteen's amazing song "Jersey Girl." "Tonight I'm going to take that ride across (Heartbreak Hill) to the (Chestnut Hill) side. Take my baby to the carnival, and then I will take on all the rides. Because down the shore, everything is all right, you and your baby on a Saturday night. You know all my dreams come true when I'm walking down the street with you... I am in love with a (BC) girl. You know she thrills me with all her charms when I'm wrapped up in my baby's arms. My little girl gives me everything; I know someday she'll wear my ring. So don't bother me man, I got no time, I'm on my way to see that girl of mine. Because nothing matters in the whole wide world when you're in love with a (BC) girl."

I have never stopped loving her in this way in well over 30 years now. Laurel is the best. Her parents raised a wonderful and gorgeous daughter. But God made her amazing. Jackson Browne's "That Girl Could Sing" is playing in the background as I type this. "She was a friend to me when I needed one. If it wasn't for her, I don't know what I would have done. She gave me back something that was missing from me."

Her beauty shines from the inside and radiates out. Laurel quite literally has a glow about her. I have often wondered if God sent us the angel that she is. I know that I am hardly worthy to be bestowed such a great treasure as her. Therefore, I must give some of my treasure to all of you to even the scales of life a bit.

I hope you enjoy this historical tale and tidbits from a life fairly well lived. I could have done better, I could have done worse, but overall I feel I'm still a work in progress. Figuring things out as I go, so to speak. The great Kenny Rogers song "The Gambler" describes what I'm talking about here well. "... And somewhere in the darkness; the Gambler, he broke even."

In this work, I have been inspired by The Secret (1982) by Byron Preiss, and Masquerade (1979) by Kit Williams. Their great treasure searches very likely inspired Forrest Fenn in his The Thrill of the Chase (2010). Forrest Fenn was spectacular and a great inspiration to me, and so many others.

I also love Phillips Exeter's own Dan Brown's incredible DaVinci Code book series and those amazing Tom Hanks movies. The Codex, The Book of the Dead, and Cities of Gold are my favorite books by the incredibly cool author Douglas Preston. He also now works with author Lincoln Child in their Pendergast mystery series of books.

This work is more of a fun life memoir based on facts that I learned or lived through. It is also an effort to preserve history. If any of the facts are wrong or incorrect, I'm sorry but "God knows I tried." So this book is historical fiction because we were not there for most of it, so we learned all from second hand sources.

I try hard to be either historically accurate or deliberately deceptive to make this treasure hunt or chase challenging. Author Douglas Preston warned me that people are really smart, and may solve your treasure hunt very quickly so be wise and make it difficult. I believe Mr. Preston is correct about this. He gave author Forrest Fenn similar advice, and his treasure was found within 10 years.

In this work, you will have to try to figure out which is an honest fact, hint, or clue, and what is a pirate's deception to keep his treasures hidden from you. It is important to remember that pirates are greedy, and want to keep their treasures hidden from the world. Before anyone asks trying to seek some special hint or clue, my treasure hunts are from the front cover to back cover, and everything in between.

My academic credentials are limited to programs related to serving in Muncipal Government Service. I sometimes joke that I'm a graduate of "Boston Beanpot University" because I have received formal education from all of these great hockey schools.

"The Beanpot" is such a great hockey tournament. If you have not gone yet, you should definitely get tickets and attend sometime. I guarantee you will not be disappointed. All four schools are equally amazing in their own special ways.

I spent about eight years full time in college. All my history knowledge I learned by studying it all the way back to Adams Elementary School (now called Waldorf School in East Lexington, Massachusetts) where they proudly taught us children all about the American Revolution.

I attended a three-week in-residence PERF senior government leaders program taught by Harvard University Business School, John F. Kennedy School of Government, and PERF Staff. These professors were amazing, and it was my honor to earn a professional certification from PERF.

Harvard University was a critical location in the American Revolution in 1775 and 1776. Harvard men also joined the Harvard Regiment 20th Massachusetts Infantry Regiment including Colonel Oliver Wendell

Holmes, Jr (a future Supreme Court Justice) to fight for the Union during the US Civil War.

It was not easy to complete my education. My parents could not help, and since I worked, I got little to no financial aid. I grew up a poor, tough kid in a rich town. Kids would bully or disrespect me, and others around me looking for fights. It is never a wise move to test the Fighting Irish   .

If you have ever seen the great Matt Damon and Ben Affleck movie "Good Will Hunting," you would understand. As I grew up, I rode those Red Line trains; behaved like Will Hunting, and got into so many fights while searching for my version of Skylar. She did not go to Harvard, rather Boston College, and she saved my life. I was completely lost until I found Laurel or she found me.

In 1981, I received a Pell grant for my freshman year of college in '81 for $500. I was so appreciative. That $500 made a big difference. So did the US Treasury Bond that my great Irish born Aunt Susan Doherty left me as an inheritance. It had matured and was valued at about $400. That was very kind of Aunt Susan, who sadly lost her life to awful diabetes in '73. I still visit her grave over 51 years later at Westview Cemetery in Lexington near the Bedford line. My whole family is in that cemetery, and so many other people that I loved in my life. May they all, rest in peace.

I was able to get guaranteed student loans from the old Coolidge Bank Mass Ave East Lexington, and paid as I went every two weeks after I matriculated at Northeastern University Boston.

They didn't seem to care that I was paying late; as long as I kept waiting in line at the Bursar's Office, and paid them every couple of weeks whatever I could including the late fee.

It was a hard world in the 60's, 70's & 80's, and I had to work for all I had. The message was well understood. I left my parent's home with the t-shirt on my back; and not much else, except a brave strong heart.

My formal education was all completed in the Boston area throughout my life. So yes, I "parked the car at Harvard yard," and I'm trying to be "wicked smart" with my thick Irish Boston accent.

Boston City of Champions Flag in my son's room (photograph by Michael O'Connell)

Go Sox, Go Pat's, Go Bruins, and Let's Go Celtics with 18 Championships!!! I am proudly wearing my 2013 Boston Strong Red Sox replica Championship ring as I type this work. I think I will leave this treasure for you to find as well. There is definitely a piece of my heart; and soul in the treasures for you all who have the time, and courageous spirit to seek it.

Let's go Boston!!! In my head, "I'm Shipping up to Boston" by Dropkick Murphys is cranked up. This was one of my younger brother John's favorite tunes. He loved all the local sports teams and all the big games, then those amazing Boston Championship parades.

My son Ryan wears a Celtics coat with pride at his current home in Los Angeles in the cold weather. Lucky young man got to watch LeBron James break Bill Russell's all-time points-scored record. Ryan is a huge Celtics fan, and was Captain of his Andover High School basketball team. Ryan is a great soccer player, too.

I admire actors Ben Affleck, Matt Damon, and the Wahlberg Brothers. Why? Because they are Boston "Townies." I have enjoyed all their movies and TV shows. I also want to acknowledge Denzel Washington for his great acting in "Glory" and "The Equalizer." Both movies had scenes filmed in Massachusetts. Denzel is, in short, amazing! Watch all their movies; you won't be disappointed. The Glory Brigade - 54th Massachusetts Regiment Sculpture on the Boston Common is breathtaking. Go visit it if you are near the Boston Common or State House. May the Glory Brigade's courage never be forgotten.

Glory Regiment 54th Massachusetts Sculpture on Boston Common (NPS Public Domain)

If you're in Boston in the summer, please go to the Cathedral of Boston - Fenway Park, or maybe grab a burger at Wahlburger's on Brookline Ave. That's Mark Wahlberg's restaurant, and he is a tremendous fan of all Boston sport teams. I'm sure the game is on the TV monitors, if you can't get Red Sox tickets. What a super cool "Townie" Mark Wahlberg is! He regularly attended mass with us at Saint Robert's Andover when he filmed his Lowell-based movie "The Fighter." Need I say more, what a great man! Father Rick Conway befriended Mark, who put him as an extra in the film walking a dog down a Lowell hill. I love that movie. Lowell is a great city to visit with lots of good places to eat.

Another Superbowl victory (Courtesy of the New England Patriots)

Regarding Quarterback Tom Brady, he is the GOAT! The Greatest QB of All Time! Coach Bill Belichick is also the Greatest NFL Coach ever. I'm proud of Rob Gronkowski, too, for winning with the Pat's then Buc's, well done! A friend of mine, Geoffrey "Buck" Buchanan, has been a Patriot's season ticket holder for many years. Buck generally calls it right because he knows the game. Another friend of ours, Steve Herrera, loves college football. He watches all the games, but I'm rarely interested in any team other than the Boston College Eagles, and Notre Dame Fighting Irish.

I am a 4th Degree Knight of Columbus and belong to the Ancient Order of Hibernians. I am very proud to be an Irish Catholic, and a son of two nations. I'm a proud son of Lexington, Massachusetts. So my Boston Irish, and New England bias is right up front. If you're still reading, likely you just smiled and are okay with this.

Nevertheless, remember I am allowed to try to deceive you or throw you off track like a crafty pirate because it's my treasure hunt and it's meant to be a fun, difficult challenge, and journey. No one will get rich in this treasure hunt but they should have have fun; and create treasured memories with their family, and friends. Jolly good! Please try to "do a good turn daily" and "do your best."

Troop 79 Andover Honor Board (created by Assistant Scoutmaster Dr. Jeremy Moses)

Scouting is a great program for young people and their parents. As an Assistant Scoutmaster, it taught me well enough to drive all the way across the United States to the Rocky Mountains. I camped and hiked from New Mexico north to Montana then into the Black Hills of South Dakota. It was a great experience. God truly blessed the United States with its majestic natural beauty. So please enjoy it all, and protect it for future generations.

My son and I met Forrest Fenn in Santa Fe, New Mexico (photograph by Brendan O'Connell)

Brendan and I met Forrest Fenn at Collected Works in Santa Fe, New Mexico in May 2018. We spoke, laughed and smiled for about an hour. Forrest made a great impression that I will never forget.

I was quite certain that he wanted his The Thrill of the Chase treasure hunt to go on, and on for over 100 years. That did not happen; Forrest Fenn's bronze chest was likely found by Labor Day 2019 by a really smart guy.

The Fenn treasure finder deserved credit for locating the chest by catching Forrest's interview slips and by perhaps reading Marvin Fenn's newspaper fishing logs housed in the archives in the Temple, Texas Public Library. This is proof that seeking treasure often begins with careful library research, as Indiana Jones stated as a professor in his famous movies. I feel that all the Indiana Jones movies inspired me but I particularly like "Indiana Jones and the Last Crusade." That scene in the Venice Library is one of my favorites!

Watch all the Indiana Jones movies to help get the mindset (photo courtesy of Lucasfilm Ltd.)

Remember to please be respectful, discreet, and leave no trace behind wherever you travel. Please be a good citizen, carry in, carry out, and clean up litter anywhere you find it. Thank you in advance.

So in 2023, I decided to do the right thing, and the fun thing to pick up where my friend Forrest Fenn left off. "The mantle has been passed to a new generation (John F. Kennedy)." Forrest gave me written permission to use his words, pictures, or images from his books, if I ever wrote myself. He did specify that I had to be respectful of him and his Chase.

That's my honor; because I loved Forrest like a distant Uncle, and still miss him. I greatly respected his military service for our nation. His achievements were truly amazing. I am humbled and honored to have known him.

I hope Forrest and his family members look down from the stars, and smile upon me and on everyone else that decides to try Lady Liberty's Treasure Hunt or Chase.   I am also writing a young adults reader called Riley's Treasure Chase. In that book, I am the crafty pirate, and my dog Riley is my compatriot.

This beautiful morning in June 2023; I suddenly became sad because I managed to drop, and smash my Fennborie coffee mug with Forrest's image on it. Dang it, too bad, I loved that coffee cup. I wonder if that was Forrest's spirit reaching out to me from his final resting place in Santa Fe to warn me to use caution; as I proceed, and prepare. Or was the deeper meaning that we should not waste time; because life is so beautiful yet fragile, and fleeting?

Paul Revere started his immortal ride in Charlestown (Public Domain)

I know a Pulitzer Award-winning writer and really great man, Dr. David Hackett Fischer, Professor Emeritus of Brandeis University History Department. I purchased signed copies of his amazing books Albion's Seed, Paul Revere's Ride, and Washington's Crossing. I have attended his history talks, and author book signings. He is, in short, spectacular. What a truly amazing, accomplished author Dr. Fischer is. Read his books; you will greatly enjoy them.

Dr. Fischer and I have chatted several times about US Colonial Times, the American Revolution, the United States Civil War, and WW2. He is a very busy man but extremely thoughtful, and kind with his time to students of history.

Dr. Fischer said to me at his beautiful Weston home, surrounded by history books in his amazing library that "I should write, and it's not too late." I responded that though I was well educated, I was not a formal historian. He said plainly, "I am a historian, Michael, and you are a historian, too." He knew full well how important 1775 to 1865 were in American history. Dr. Fischer then said, "Michael, you need to find the time to write and pass on your knowledge to the next generation, or the information you possess may be lost to time."

When I returned to my home that night, I looked around my own fairly large library of history books, collectibles, and art prints. I realized our similar interests, and that Dr. Fischer was correct. I wanted to follow Dr. Fischer's charge to me but thought some folks don't really care about history too much. How could I teach them just a little bit about history, and make it fun and interesting?

Then I immediately thought of Forrest Burke Fenn, my friend, who managed to get me to study New Mexico, Colorado, Wyoming, Yellowstone National Park, and Montana history for hundreds of hours. Forrest may not have realized it, but he was indirectly teaching perhaps 300,000 people about Southwestern United States history in his The Thrill of the Chase, Too Far to Walk, Once Upon a Star, and other books. I own almost every book Forrest Fenn wrote.

Forrest Fenn referred to himself as "Mr. Southwest," and he called famous painter Eric Sloane of Warren, Connecticut, "Mr. Northeast." Encouraged by Forrest, I own a bunch of Eric Sloane's beautiful signed books, and prints. I have driven through the Massachusetts Berkshires, rural New York, gorgeous Connecticut Covered Bridges near his former home in Warren, Vermont Mountains, scenic New Hampshire, and Adams & Bucks County Pennsylvania scenic areas where Eric Sloane did so many of his well-known Covered Bridge and Rustic Barn artworks.

You may locate Eric Sloane's Spirit of '76 Bell (photograph by Michael O'Connell)

My wife and I visited the Eric Sloane Museum in Kent, CT. It is worth a visit with your family, friends, or loved ones. I own some of the gorgeous prints in their nice collection. We visited Sloane's old home in Warren and saw the Cornwall Bridge he so often painted. On top of Eric Sloane's Museum, there is a bell with a long cord so children may ring it every year on July 4th. Eric loved bells, weathervanes, barns, and covered bridges. He wrote books and completed paintings about all of them. So go there, and find the bell. Ask the Museum Staff if your children can ring the bell to remember Eric Sloane and his best friend Forrest Fenn. They both "Remembered America," and we all should, too.

Connecticut still has three historic covered bridges. They are like the famous movie scenes in the "Bridges of Madison County" that starred Clint Eastwood and Meryl Streep. It's a safe bet Eric Sloane visited all of these bridges doing his work. Some of them are in his famous artworks, and in his books. They are worth a visit if you like history or scenic spots.

Perhaps Eric Sloane's most famous work is the giant wall mural at the Smithsonian Air and Space Museum at Dulles Airport, Virginia. I stopped there in my tracks once for about a half hour in absolute awe. What a great museum, I have visited it perhaps three or four times.

Eric Sloane was a treasure to his nation, if not to all of his wives. Eric Sloane is said to have stated in jest: "That his ex-wives were all housekeepers because every time he got divorced, they kept the house." He was a great painter, if not such a great husband to those first few wives. His last wife is buried with him, so she must have been more patient or understanding. My wife Laurel definitely has these great qualities, especially for putting up with this time-consuming, and expensive writing project.

Webb-Deane-Stevens Museum Old Wethersfield (Public Domain)

Annual Memorial Day reenactment at Old Wethersfield (Courtesy of 5th Connecticut Reg't)

Another great American treasure, that I visited on Memorial Day weekend a few years ago for their annual Revolutionary War Encampment is the Webb-Deane-Stevens Museum 211 Main St. Wethersfield, CT. John Adams visited Deane House (circa 1770) in 1774. General George Washington was also there in 1775 while on his way to assume command of the Continental Army conducting the seige of Boston.

Memorial Day American Revolution Encampment (courtesy of 5th Connecticut Regiment)

The Joseph Webb House was built in 1752. General George Washington met on May 21 - 22, 1781 with French Army General Rochambeau. Here the two men (with Washington in overall command) planned out some of their military campaign, and joint operations of the French and Continental Armies. Their overall actions would lead to British General Cornwallis' Surrender at Yorktown, and the eventual American victory that led to freedom from British rule.

If you are in Connecticut, perhaps stop and tour Choate School with your school age children. This is where President John F. Kennedy went to school before Harvard. Many believe a headmaster at this school inspired JFK's famous inauguration speech line: "Ask not what your country can do for you, ask what you can do for your country."

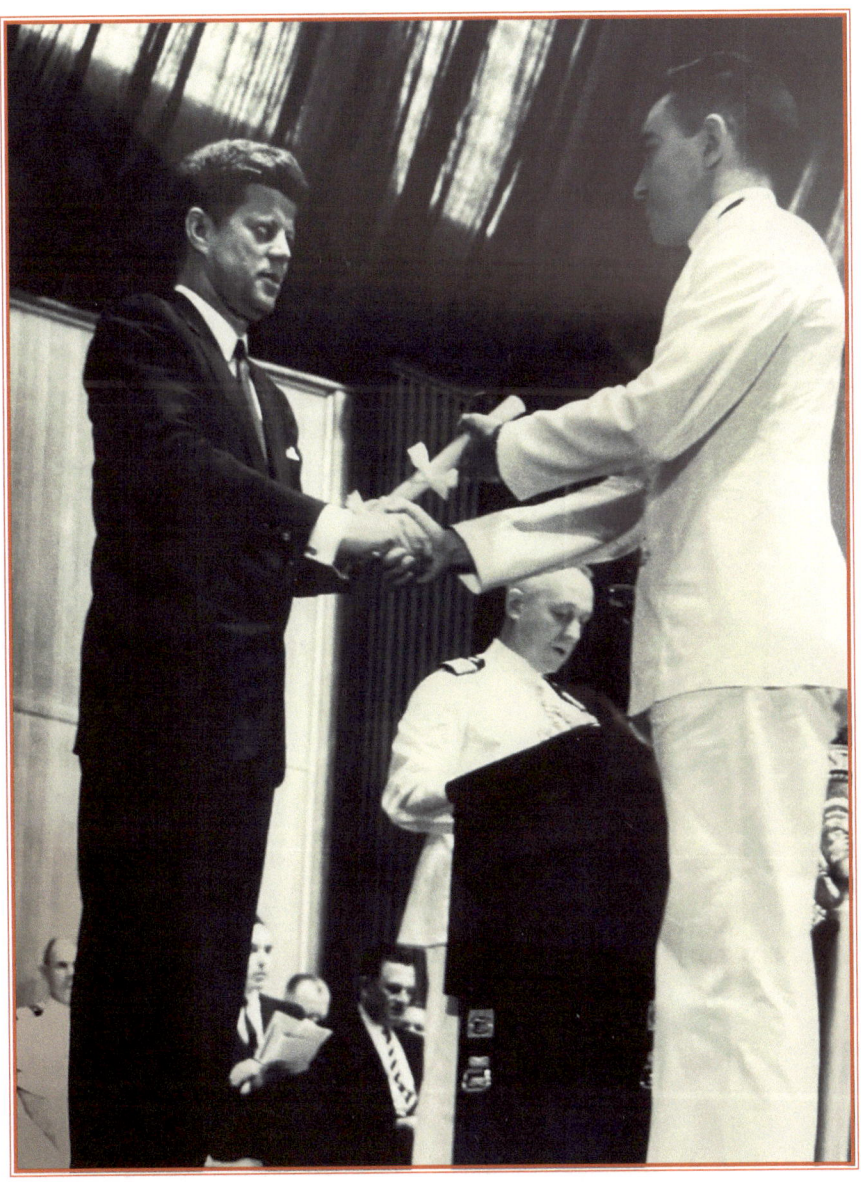

President Kennedy at the United States Naval Academy 1961

This great charge by the First Irish Catholic US President shaped my entire life. I cannot do enough for my community, state, or nation. My wife has also served her nation faithfully for over 30 years. I commend her and those like her in public service. Thank you to all who serve our nation, and those who have answered President John F. Kennedy's charge.

Eric Sloane begins his CT drive on a Road to Taos (courtesy of owner of this Cornwall artwork)

Now back to Forrest Fenn's great Connecticut friend, Eric Sloane. I have a signed copy of his famous book: "The Road to Taos." So I decided to mimic Eric Sloane's Road to Taos by driving in 2018 from New England to scenic Warren, Cornwall Bridge, Connecticut, to Brooklyn, New York, Buck's County, and Adams County Pennsylvania area, then on the road to Taos, New Mexico. Then I met Forrest Fenn at The Collected Works Bookstore in Santa Fe, New Mexico.

Artist Eric Sloane in his studio (courtesy of Eric Sloane Museum Kent, Connecticut)

I was Remembering America as Eric Sloane had done so long before me. I hope Eric and Forrest are together in heaven having a good laugh. Perhaps they are looking down on me as I try to respectfully continue their efforts to preserve our national memories of those who have gone before us.

Forrest Fenn's heart was amazing, and he meant well, but several mistakes by others hurt his great Chase. Folks are not supposed to die treasure hunting. I reached out to famous writer Doug Preston for further advice. I love his writing, and have a bunch of his books in my library. He was very close to Forrest Fenn. I told Mr. Preston about more about my Northeast Treasure Hunt plans. Mr. Doug Preston said that I should try to make any "treasure hunt as difficult as possible." He added that: "there are a lot of really smart people out there." He had now repeated this advice to me twice for good reason, and I will try hard to follow it.

Doug Preston told me that he gave Forrest Fenn the same advice before he launched his treasure hunt in 2010. Within a decade, Forrest's bronze chest was located. This seemed to disappoint Forrest somewhat.

I think Forrest Fenn was hoping his chase would keep going on and on in the years ahead. Forrest should have been proud that some 300,000 people reportedly searched for his treasure but most of them were really just taking family vacations. That's the best part of the journey, enjoying time with family or friends. That's why I'm creating my treasure chases, too. So folks enjoy time with their family and friends, while learning a bit about the past. Therefor, everyone wins in this quest.

I have done my best to avoid any of *The Thrill of the Chase* or *Masquerade* treasure hunt difficulties but who can guess the future, certainly not I. Treasure hunting is no easy task. If you are in the right spot, a very discrete use of copper divining rods may help you. Be wise, and don't get yourself in trouble. If you do get in trouble; that trouble is yours, and no one else is responsible. So please use your head. We don't want any of the problems that The Thrill of the Chase Treasure Hunt faced because of searchers' lack of commonsense.

Lady Liberty's treasure is not near my current residence, so please don't visit without an appointment. Pestering anyone will definitely not help any treasure searcher. My home has no hints or clues in it. Please be wise and respectful, and do not call or visit my home without specific permission from me. I will leave an email address in the book for thoughtful correspondence but negative messages will not be answered, and will be politely deleted.

Please don't spend money that you don't have on this Treasure Hunt or Chase. Also, please don't get so obsessed that you destroy any of your relationships. Use common sense please. Further, don't walk, hike or bike beyond your fitness levels please. There is always another opportunity to hike, bike, or search for my treasures. Yes, it may take more than one vacation to be successful in this game. Folks made repeated trips in other treasure hunts. Likely, this will require the same effort.

Heartbreaks in treasure hunting are quite normal; heart attacks or injuries, not so much. No swimming or diving is necessary. My treasures are not deliberately under water. So please don't drown, fall off cliffs or embankments, or crash your mountain bike or get hit crossing any street or roadway. Any police officer would politely ask you to please always drive your car safely, never overtired, distracted, or going too fast. Please take appropriate breaks for safety's sake. Keep hydrated; bring bug spray, check for ticks if you're in the woods or in fields or meadows.

Any Treasure Hunt or Chase takes time, effort, and patience, so please don't hurry. This Treasure Hunt is "Too Far to Walk" like Forrest Fenn's treasure hunt, and you definitely need a car to go to many of these places covered in the Northeast states.

Please remember no locations south of Pennsylvania or New Jersey are included in this treasure hunt or chase. That means West Virginia, Washington D.C., Maryland, and Delaware are not included in the search area. Please check the weather before you go out for the day. No one wants to get struck by lightning or get caught in a downpour.

Crosswalks and bridges were built for a reason. So if you want to row a boat or kayak, that's really fun but I strongly doubt it will help you find a Lady Liberty's Treasure Hunt chest. My treasures are not hidden in a cave or deep steep drops, or under a water body or on top of a mountain. There should be absolutely no safety risks searching for my treasures. If there are any safety risks, you are not being prudent.

Treasure hunters should try to always fit in, like a tourist or hiker, biker, and not draw unnecessary attention to them. "If you find a treasure, I give you title to it (Forrest Fenn)." If you find a treasure, please take it quietly, and discreetly from the area. Please leave no trace behind that you were ever there. That's an important scouting, hiking, mountain biking or camping principle we all should follow.

The treasure chest will have instructions in it to help you earn a further reward by contacting me. I strongly suggest you follow them precisely as part of this fun game. In short, always be prepared and try not to get into any trouble. "So tarry scant with marvel gaze, just take your chest and go in peace (Forrest Fenn)."

From cover to cover, all of the places in this work are in play in Lady Liberty's Treasure Hunt or Chase. I have visited all of the described locations in my wonderful though humble life. If you cross into New Jersey and Pennsylvania, you are still in treasure states, but states south of them are out of bounds in this treasure hunt. To me, Bruce Springsteen is the greatest treasure from NJ. His music with the E Street Band was beyond amazing. Please play "Jungle Land" and "Thunder Road" in honor of the Boss and his timeless band.

I have been active as an adult leader in Scouting for over 25 years. I can easily drive my car great distances, take my mountain bike off the bike rack, and go for a short or long ride. For example, I hiked 8 miles yesterday, and biked 12 miles today. I am really fit; have hiked great distances with my backpack, and water bottles full. "Just heavy loads and water high. (Forrest Fenn)."

Scout troops will do well in my Treasure Hunts or Chases because they like the outdoors, and persistent challenges. My youngest son Corey is an Eagle Scout, completing every rank from Tiger Scout over 12 years. My other children were all in scouting too for varying years.

Four Troop 79 Eagle Scouts at MNP with their proud Dads (photograph by Jason Webber)

Corey and his close friend Matthew Webber created and built the Pleasant Brook Trail off Pleasant St in Andover. Corey's part was a 260-foot boardwalk bridge over wetlands. His friend and fellow Eagle Scout Robert Pothier joked: "You have to pay a toll to the Troll to cross his bridge." I would add to Robert's advice if you see the Troll try to make him smile, and follow his gaze. Robert's father Rob Pothier is a great friend, and Assistant Scoutmaster of Troop 79. Matthew's father Jason Webber is a dear friend, Eagle Scout, and former Assistant Scoutmaster, too.

My oldest son Brendan proudly exclaimed that he earned his BSA Arrow of Light Badge and then crossed into Troop 79 as his youngest brother made Eagle Scout. I'm truly proud to have served in Scouting adult leadership. As a team of committed parents, we helped so many young folks get a great start in life.

Brendan was a three-sport athlete at Phillips Academy Andover, and very active in student organizations. He just got too busy for Troop 79. Fair enough Brendan eventually earned a Sarah Lawrence degree, then an Ivy League degree at Columbia University of New York City.

Brendan loved his time at Phillips Academy Andover. Brendan and his classmates were going off to conquer the world, with Katy Perry's song "Firework" inspiring them to pursue their dreams.

Not too shabby. His great-grandmother Mary Ann Doherty fled religious oppression and poverty in Strabane, Northern Ireland. She got off a steerage class section of the Columbia ship in the early 1900s at Ellis Island New York Harbor, and he graduated from a prestigious school with the same name in the same city. That's the American dream actually coming true. If my grandmother had not been so brave, neither Brendan nor I would exist. Thank you for everything, Grandma!

The Bell Tower at Phillips Academy was built to honor all those former students that were lost in WW1 on those truly sad battlefields in Europe. When the bell tolls, it remembers all those who served our nation all the way back to the French Indian Wars.

Lady Liberty's Treasure Hunt or Chase remembers them all as well. They gave us this great nation; all of those tremendously brave folks. Freedom is not free. People gave their lives so all of us could live free. We should never ever forget them, and what they fought for.

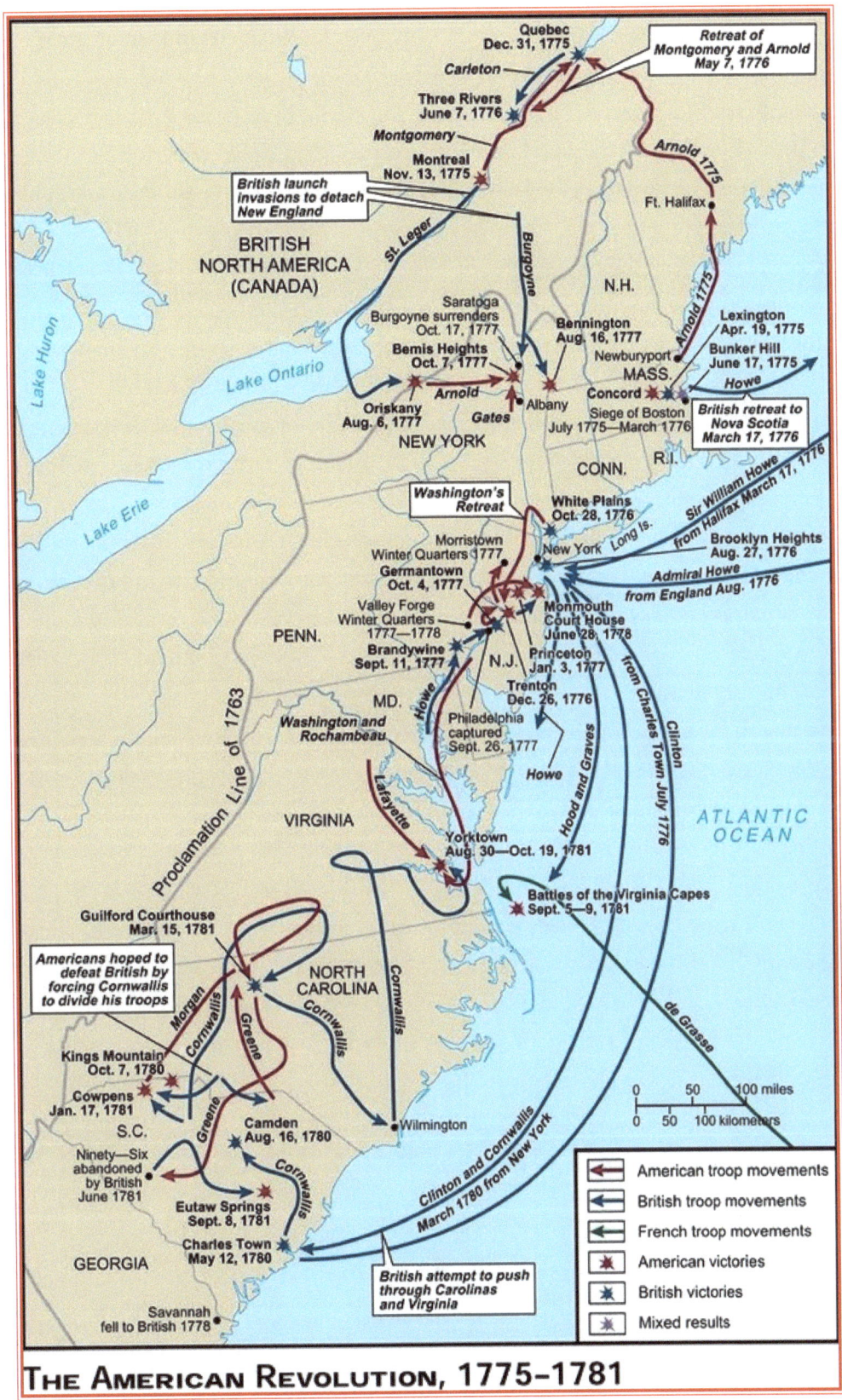

THE AMERICAN REVOLUTION, 1775–1781

Area of the American Revolution Battles on Land (Public Domain)

President George Washington visited Andover on his great campaign ride so long ago. A granite marker points out this very special place by the WW1 Bell Tower. Washington was an outstanding General, and is a great leader to closely study. He was not a perfect man; those who lived in his time had great faults.

If you make the ride out here sometime to see Phillips Academy Andover with your children, maybe they can apply to attend there if you value a great education. Set up a tour for your children with Admissions. Then when you do the campus tour, please ask them about the Bell Tower.

There is a great place to eat close by Bartlet St Cafe at 11 Bartlet St Andover. Go visit Nick and Jenny Macheras for their healthy meal options. Their sons were also in BSA Troop 79, and one of them made Eagle Scout. Nick and Jenny were active adult leaders in Andover Pack 79 and Troop 79. They made a great difference in young peoples lives, and are great friends. My family and I eat there often.

Now it is time to get ready to learn a bit; and have a whole lot of great fun with your family, and friends. If you keep a positive attitude, you may find one of Lady Liberty's awesome treasures. You must be 18 to participate for safety's sake, so please get a trusted adult to take you treasure hunting if you're under 18.

Please get off the couch, ask your friends to buy a book, discuss it, then get out there in the sunshine. My grandfather Michael Cloherty in County Galway, Ireland used to say, "Don't let the rain bother you, Lad. It will only make your hair grow." I would add to that to always look for the rainbow after the rain stops. Perhaps it will lead you to a treasure, Lassie. Remember I'm Irish, so I believe in Connemara Leprechauns, seeking out rainbows, and finding treasure.

Spending time with my cute Cavapoo dog Riley, hiking or riding my mountain bike relieves all my stress. I only have to reward Riley with water and a few treats once in a while. So please don't be stressed or stress others out with negative energy on social media or blogs because there is no reward in that stuff.

Remember there are no treasure hunting so-called experts. Your ideas are just as good as the next person's. Just stay positive and never stop searching. Smile, and the world will smile back at you.

On Father's Day '23, my cute little Riley dog climbed up in bed with me; and cuddled in my arm, with his head resting on my left shoulder. This is his favorite place to be. Riley was happily snoring away as the sun rose. My wife got up early, and I could smell the coffee waiting but I resisted its attraction. With Riley now 14, and with serious heart disease, I realized it was very likely his last Father's Day with me.

Riley is immortalized in Riley's Treasure Chase book (photo by Brendan O'Connell)

Sad face, I honestly love Riley so very much. All my kids are adults and off doing their thing. Riley waits patiently for me until I get home, gives me unconditional love, and never likes to be parted from me. Nothing on this planet can love you more than a dog. When you spell dog backwards, what do you get? I really don't think that is a coincidence.

I let Riley happily sleep in, warmly cuddling my arm, and enjoyed the extra time with him. I'm sure going to miss my best friend when he decides it's time to go. Carpe Diem - seize the moment. Don't let time slip away.

Lady Liberty's Treasure Hunt or Chase will get you some good healthy fresh air, exercise, or fun. So roll down your car windows, bring John Denver's and Bob Seger's greatest hits with you, hit those "Country Roads," and "Roll Clean Out of Sight."

Find your way, take a family fun road trip, take photos, and make many safe stops along the way. All of the New England states are in play, as are New York, New Jersey, and Pennsylvania. I created a map in this book to help folks on their journey.

My children love to play board games when they are home for the holidays or vacation weeks. It's always special for my wife and me when our older children travel home from the far-off places they now reside. They often shake their heads at me because in the winter months, I enjoy watching "Game of Thrones" or "House of the Dragons" series. I have seen every episode multiple times. I love to binge-watch the "West Wing" Series, too.

Please see Tom Berringer & Martin Sheen in Gettysburg film (Courtesy of Ted Turner TNT)

Martin Sheen is an amazing actor. I loved his acting as Confederate General Robert E. Lee in the 1993 famous movie "Gettysburg" based on Michael Shaara's "The Killer Angels." I own this book and enjoy its detailed storytelling of one of the most significant battles in American history. I've met his son, Jeff Shaara, and obtained signed copies of his books. I have a comprehensive library of US Civil War, American Revolutionary War, and World War II books.

Maine's greatest US Civil War hero Joshua Chamberlain (Public Domain)

Gettysburg is a must-watch Ted Turner film, and The Killer Angels won the Pulitzer Prize. Jeff Daniels portrayed General Joshua Chamberlain, the hero of Little Round Top and Maine's greatest hero. On July 2, 1863 the 20th Maine ran out of ammunition. Most leaders would have retreated but not Chamberlain. He crossed his arms, stood his ground, ordered his men to fix bayonets, and then commanded them to charge. They won this days battle and Chamberlain earned the Medal of Honor. He would later serve as Maine's Governor, and President of Bowdoin College. There are at least 4 monuments dedicated to Chamberlain or his beloved 20th Maine Regiment. An amazing man to study closely. I own a document he signed long ago, what a treasure.

Brian Mallon played Major General Winfield Hancock, a proud son of Pennsylvania and a significant Union Civil War hero. There's a well-deserved statue of him at Gettysburg on Cemetery Hill. Hancock saved the Army of the Potomac by heroically fighting for three straight days until he was shot. I wish he had dismounted when Lee attacked his position, but Hancock was too brave, inspiring his men from horseback as Joshua Chamberlain looked on in awe.

I own a document General Hancock signed after the war as well. He was the Democratic Candidate for President of the United States but lost in a close popular vote election to President Garfield. Garfield was Lt. Colonel in the 42nd Ohio Infantry during the US Civil War. President Garfield sadly was shot by an assasin on July 2, 1881 at the Baltimore and Potomac Railroad Station in Washington D.C. He died that September.

Irish Brigade Reenactor & Civil War Author Brian Pohanka 1955 – 2005 (Public Domain)

The Irish won two wars at once (photograph by Michael O'Connell)

Hancock's Irish Brigade once again served with great honor at Gettysburg. May they never be forgotten. God bless Ireland!

This Gettysburg Union Irish Monument was made by a former CSA Irish soldier (Public Domain)

Stay and Fight It Out by Don Stivers (Courtesy of donstivers.com)

General George Meade arrived at the Leister House at Gettysburg late on July 1, 1863, and said it was so dark he couldn't see a darn thing.

Union Major General Meade's Headquarters at Gettysburg (photo by Michael O'Connell)

With Generals Warren, Slocum, and Hunt at his disposal, he had a treasure trove of great leaders. Meade might not have known what to do until Slocum spoke. Meade wisely asked his Corps Commanders for their opinions. General Henry Slocum said, "Let's stay and fight it out," then Hancock and the other Generals present agreed. Meade gave General Henry Hunt full discretion on where to deploy his artillery on July 2nd and 3rd.

It was brilliant and truly sad how effective Hunt's cannon were at Malvern Hill, Sharpsburg, and Gettysburg. Hunt and his men made a significant difference in achieving a Union victory, and none of them died in vain. Between General Slocum and General Hunt; the two Henry's, how could you go wrong? General George Meade was a smart Union Commander, took his subordinate's advise, beat CSA General Robert E. Lee at Gettysburg, and is a true American hero.

I located General Meades, Lee's, Hood's, Hampton's, and Longstreet's autographs many years ago to add them to my collection. But I had trouble locating Generals Hunt and Slocum's autographs. In 2024 I finally got these, what a treasure between the two!

If anyone has a General John Buford, General John Reynolds, CSA General Harry Heth, or General A.P. Hill signed document please email me, and I want to add them to my collection. I like to bring real items such as signed documents, art prints, swords, buckles, revolvers, rifles and muskets to teach folks about US history 1770 to 1945. I collect from all these era's to teach folks effectively.

I recommend watching the movie "Gettysburg" on July 1 to get an idea of the hot weather those men faced on that sad but great Civil War Battle Field. I've visited there numerous times, and absolutely love Gettysburg. I can't wait to go back again!

American Revolutionary War hero Light Horse Harry Lee Governor of Virginia (Public Domain)

General Robert E. Lee was the son of "Light Horse" Harry Lee, a favorite of General George Washington in the Cavalry arm of the service during the American Revolution. I few years back I purchased a cool signed document by Henry Lee when he was Governor of Virginia. What a treasure! He was a great hero to our young nation.

In 1778, Light Horse Harry Lee won the famous Battles of Paulus Hook in New Jersey, and at Edgar's Lane Hastings by the Hudson Village near historic Dobbs Ferry, New York. The Village of Sleepy Hollow, New York, is only six miles away; one of the Hessians beheaded by Light Horse Harry Lee's Cavalry must be responsible for chasing down Ichabod Crane in Washington Irving's "The Legend of Sleepy Hollow."

Inchabod's Chase Legend of Sleepy Hollow, NY (Public Domain)

Interestingly, Confederate General Robert E. Lee's father rebelled against King George III in the American colonies. Henry Lee was brave, and aggressive. For his victorious campaigns, Light Horse Harry was promoted to Lt. Colonel, and the Continental Congress presented him with a gold medal for his actions at Paulus Hook.

US Army Lt. of Engineers Robert E. Lee 1838 (Public Domain)

Robert E. Lee also rebelled against the National Government; showing the same bravery, and aggression as his father in the Mexican War. It's unfortunate that the sons fought against what their fathers had won, and that the C.S.A. fought for four years to preserve slavery. What a sad, and terrible thing to fight for.

I wish Robert E. Lee had accepted President Abraham Lincoln's offer to Command the Union Army prior to the Battle of Bull Run at Manassas, Virginia. I believe this may have shortened that terrible war; that cost at least 600,000 American lives, by two years.

Presidents Grant, Ford and Eisenhower later forgave Robert E. Lee for his grave faults. President Ford signed the law that restored Robert E. Lee's US Citizenship in 1975, and General Eisenhower purchased a farm at Gettysburg, where he spent much of his second term. President Eisenhower praised Lee's character eventhough he acknowledged his major errors. The Eisenhower's Farm is a beautiful National Park Service historic property to visit. I really enjoyed it.

Longstreet & Lee led their army in retreat July 4 - 5, 1863 toward Fairfield (Gettysburg 1993)

I enjoy studying US, Irish, and European history and have donated to the American Battlefields Trust. They preserve our American Revolution and Civil War battlefields. Please check them out at www.battlefields. org if you want to help us preserve our precious US History. American Battlefields Trust also makes maps (like below example), and they teach history very well to all who wish to learn.

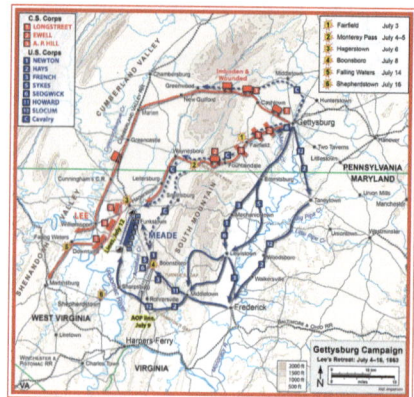

R.E. Lee's Retreat commenced July 4 – 5, 1863 (Courtesy Of American Battlefield Trust)

My children enjoy playing Risk Game of Thrones board game. I always play the "King of the North" or "Lord of the North" and I lose every time stubbornly defending the North. Because I'm always a Stark, I must fight like a "Deyerwolf." We pretend to be the actual houses, and taunt it each other with medieval slang. It's pretty funny.

House of Stark Flag (Courtesy of HBO please watch Game of Thrones & House of the Dragons)

My second son Ryan; who has a tremendous sense of humor, decided to gag-gift me at Christmas by officially naming me a Scottish Lord with a certificate. So now, I am truly the "Lord of the North." He knew I was knighted long ago as a 3rd-degree Knight of Columbus. I recently completed the 4th degree "Sir Knight" (Patriotic Order). Please support your local Knights of Columbus, and The Ancient Order of Hibernians in their charitable works in your communities.

The taunts continue, and I keep losing because I will never leave the North. In this Treasure Hunt, it would be reasonable to refer to me as "the Lord or King of the North" or "Sir Knight." As a Blue Knight, I'm sure the true King, Lord Jon Snow, and his pretended father but true uncle, Lord Eddard Stark, wouldn't mind. The Starks have a great family name, and history. They would rather live free or die. I find this series to be a true treasure, and love the House of the Dragons, too. Winter is coming for all of us so just embrace it.

Every King should have a great Queen by his side, which he worships and adores. My Queen is Laurel, her nickname in this quest is *Lady Liberty*. I love her more than anything. When I look upon her, I hear and feel the emotions in the famous British band Styx's song "Lady." So please don't do anything to upset or offend my Queen or Lady, or you will immediately feel my wrath.

Maybe King Charles III or William, Prince of Wales, will read this book and make me a Member of the "Order of the Garter" and an Irish or Scottish Lord so my wife Laurel can become an official Lady. She truly deserves it after raising four children and fighting off cancer over the past years. She is amazing and should have married a Prince of men instead of me. I truly do not deserve so fair of a *Lady*.

We were deeply saddened to learn that Princess of Wales Catherine "Kate" Middleton is fighting cancer, too. Princess Catherine is an inspiration to all of us. She, Prince William, their children and loved ones are in our prayers. May God heal Princess Catherine quickly, and completely.

My Irish family bloodline now goes all the way back to Richard O'Connell from Fermoy, County Cork prior to 1775. I believe the great liberator of Ireland, Daniel O'Connell, is of this bloodline, too. That's pretty cool. I guess I really am entitled to be an Irish Prince after all. My mother use to call me an Irish Prince perhaps she was right?

Peaceful Stage Fort Park Gloucester, MA (City of Gloucester Public Domain)

I took my mother Brigid Cloherty O'Connell to Stage Fort Harbor, Gloucester. She looked out across the ocean toward her native home in Lettercallow, Lettermore, County Galway, Ireland. We sat looking out

MICHAEL CLOHERTY O'CONNELL

across the water on a beautiful warm day. Sadly, that was the last time my mother saw the Atlantic Ocean. She appreciated that Bing Crosby sang "Galway Bay" on national television. She loved that song so much. I hope Brigid Cloherty O'Connell's spirit returned to Ireland before she went home to God. May God bless Ireland, and all my ancestors.

Stage Fort Park is a beautiful place to visit. You can walk down the boulevard, see the famous Fisherman's statue, enjoy beautiful gardens, and grab an ice cream. Our family loves this area so much. Enjoy all the beaches of summer whenever you can.

Since I'm royalty as "King of the North' and surrounded by gold, silver, and precious treasure, I think I will share them with those among you who are wise enough to find them. But you will have to be clever like a pirate to find one of my treasures. It's also why pirates are remembered. No one will forget Captain Black Beard, and folks still actively search for his treasure.

Commodore John Paul Jones (US Naval Academy Public Domain)

The British considered John Paul Jones akin to a marauding ruthless pirate. On the other side of the pond, he was considered a privateer, hero and one of the Fathers of the United States Navy. One person's villain is another person's hero. I guess it all depends on your perspective. The United States and France even had a coin struck in John Paul Jones's honor. His fame started in Kittery, Maine, as Captain of the Ranger. Of course, Maine used to be part of the Bay State, Massachusetts, during the American Revolution. They have a couple monuments in his memory.

Pirates scorn all property laws. If they land or visit there, the land is theirs, and they discreetly hide their treasure or take any treasure present that they find. These are wise methods of treasure hiding or hunting.

Pirates play hide and seek but do not maliciously damage property ever. They hide or seek treasure, that's it. Pirates leave their mark on this world but leave no trace behind except some blaze to help them recover their treasure.

I pay homage and give my respects to Captain Black Beard and those brave few privateers like Captain John Paul Jones. Pirate types play to win, do not play fair, and want to keep their treasure hidden forever.

The more you struggle to find my treasure, the greater the challenge and victory when you find one of my treasures full of booty. Some will be worth more than others, hidden randomly within 50 to 100 yards of their location's blaze.

If you ask me a question I don't like or get too close to my booty, I may deceive you willfully. I may then fall over laughing to myself. So you must be a swashbuckling soul, brave and clever, to beat me at my shifty Pirate's game. That is the true nature of treasure hunting. It's a time-consuming challenge but also a whole lot of good old-fashioned tourism, exercise, and fun.

You can ride ferries if you like, but they are not involved in this treasure hunt unless you live on an island and are traveling to a mainland location. Nothing against our beautiful friends to the North but Canada is out of play. So if you go that far north, please turn about. My treasure chests or caches are hidden somewhere in the USA.

Canadians, please get a passport and join the Treasure Hunt or Chase for fun. You may find a bunch of valuable Canadian Mint Maple Leaf silver or gold coins waiting for you in a treasure chest or more. Oh, Canada, I sing your praises for you are the greatest of neighbors. I'm proud to state that I have French-Canadian relatives. My wife is a French-Canadian & Irish-American beauty. Her beauty comes from the inside and radiates out. Everyone loves her. Everyone who finds her treasure will love *Lady Liberty,* too.

All of you will love her US, Canadian Mint silver, and gold coins in her treasure chests. If you find a chest and open it, I hope you feel joy, but "tarry scant with marvel gaze, just take the chest and go in peace (Forrest Fenn)." Remember to "leave no trace behind" that you were there. That's a very important principle.

I have visited all the places in this tale. But I went there alone to hide my treasure troves and kept their locations a secret. So please don't bother my family or friends. "Two people can keep a secret, if one of them is dead (Forrest Fenn)." So I told no one where I hid the treasure.

My family and friends have been instructed by me either to not respond to inquiries or to provide deliberately false information of no true value to distract or deceive those who pursue this type of annoying folly. So save your time, and energy in this regard please.

Don't bother trying to befriend me with flattery. That stuff doesn't work on salty Pirates, Knights, Lords, or Kings. Many folks who got close to Forrest Fenn likely were just looking for slips, hints, or clues. All that did was cause problems in his search; and made other treasure searchers frustrated, thinking it was unfair of Forrest Fenn to help some, and not others. Forrest had a kind soul and was just being friendly but it appears that he made verbal slips once in a while. So to be fair, I will carefully avoid such interactions as best I can, and I will not make any slips. If anyone tries to trick me or force me to give him or her information, I will deliberately deceive him or her. I hope you all understand.

It took me many years, and personal sacrifice to collect all the items in my treasure chests. I hid all of them before I released this book but won't say what year it was; except that it was sometime before 2025, 250 years after the beginning of the American Revolution. This is deliberate because I am a Lexington native. If you cut me, I would certainly bleed Lexington High School Blue and Gold or Union Blue and Irish Green. That's just who I am. I am a proud son of two countries. I love them both and honor all my ancestors in this work. Erin Go Braugh, God bless Ireland, and may God bless the United States of America.

This Treasure Hunt or Chase is about enjoying your time with others; that's all I can promise you. I can't promise you treasure, just a whole lot of fun. Life is so precious, fragile, and short. So make the most of it before Father Time or the Grim Reaper comes calling for you. "Don't fear the Reaper" by Blue Oyster Cult is softly playing in the background as I write this. So don't waste time, gather your close friends or family, buy some treasure books, and have fun living life and treasure hunting.

"As I have gone there alone; with my treasure bold, and a hint of treasures new and old. (Forrest Fenn)"

Please begin this search by becoming a time traveler. Bounce back and forth from time and place, from contemporary to old times and intertwined memories, and then back again and again. A good example of this type of time travel is Robert De Nero's famous movie *Once Upon a Time in America* (1984). He is a great actor, and I love all his movies. Another great example of this type of writing is Mario Puzo's novel; that the movie *The Godfather* (1972), was based upon.

Sadly, pianist George Winston died on June 4, 2023, as I was editing this work. After a long fight with cancer, his spirit left at age 73. My wife Laurel, and I enjoy his music. We saw him live in concert a couple of times. George Winston was absolutely amazing.

He would walk out confidently in his stocking feet with no shoes on because the shoes might impact his ability to use his foot pedals. George Winston's music revolutionized his field, and impacted a generation of artists behind him. Thank you, George, for making our world a better place. You will be missed. I hope you play your piano in heaven for a great audience of Angels.

My wife Laurel also played piano when she was younger. She loves music. We own many of George Winston's CDs, and I would often play them on long road trips with our whole family in the car. My two favorite George Winston albums are "Summer" and "Autumn." Perhaps buy those old CDs or download the music for your long road trips on the search with your family.

Somewhere between these cryptic lines is the perpetual glory of *Lady Liberty's Treasure Hunt* treasure chests. I wanted to challenge folks so each state involved may contain a treasure. That way; children from all these states, and states nearby can take some weekend trips or vacations with their parents to enjoy all the states in *Lady Liberty's Treasure Hunt* or off to Massachusetts for *Riley's Treasure Chase*. Teaching young people American history is really important to me. They are the future, so please teach them wisely.

We all seek immortality, but sadly that belongs only to God and the finder of my treasures. "Winner, winner, chicken dinner (Las Vegas, NV gambling expression)." Now get out there and have some fun. Smile, and the world will smile back at you.

Fort Ticonderoga New York (Public Domain)

The French and Indian War began around 1754 and ended with a British victory in 1763. Fort Ticonderoga (formerly called Fort Carillon by the French) in New York was involved in the French and Indian War on July 26 and 27, 1759. The American Colonists fought with the British. A British force of 11,000 under the command of General Jeffery Amherst moved artillery into place, and French General Louis Joseph de Montcalm withdrew his 400 troops. The British were pleased to capture this fort strategically abutting Lake George. I stayed at the Mohawk Campground when I was up there. Being a BSA Assistant Scoutmaster for years, I'm used to camping. Upper State New York is a nice area to visit with your family or friends.

The French and Indian Wars gave Britain supremacy in the Ohio Valley and Canada. The French and Indian Wars cost a lot of money, so the King and Parliament issued a series of taxes that led to problems in the American colonies. The French and Indian Wars also taught many Americans how to fight hit-and-run style like the Native Americans. The war also developed future leaders like Colonel George Washington.

King George III said, "the die is now cast," and told Lord Dartmouth to send General Gage to do his bidding. Like the tree blossoms growing in the warmth of Spring, the bees soon will follow, and some may well sting.

Solomon Brown got wind of a serious concern. He rode to Sgt. Munroe's home and warned him. Munroe then set up a guard to protect Adams, Hancock, and Clarke.

Start your journey at the Old South Meeting House and hear the bells toll. Then head to Griffin's Wharf for some tea. Next, visit North Square and see the oldest house in the city. It's next door to Colonel Robert Shaw's (54th Massachusetts Regiment) great-grandfather's former house, where Pitcairn was billeted. From there, go to Cyrus' mount and proudly proceed with iron resolve on a freedom trail to a journey back in time.

As the Eagle takes flight, you must travel great distances in your quest. The best treasure searchers have granite resolve and iron in their veins, so keep marching on like the hourglass, and don't get easily discouraged.

You are having fun on a great journey, but that does not mean finding a chest is your vision quest. Maybe another will be more successful; if they are, please commend and applaud them. No sore sports, please.

If you are Irish or not, wear your green proudly. Head to the Dragon, speak to the sons, and have a pint for Liberty's sake or go to Doctor's place in the shadow of the famous hill and have some fish and chips or a burger. But since you're pretty close by, visit King Street (now State St.) where the 29th Regiment took their infamous fire upon the crowd in 1770. The first massacre, another would later follow in 1775.

The Granary holds their prominent graves. The dead are buried with lime. They lie forever still, and know only that it's far better to be alive. Our opponent's foolhardy move would eventually lead to war.

The light of Newman's one lantern or perhaps more will direct you on your way. As Voight and Cage once spoke in their clever but deceptive way, for only they could claim that treasure. If you don't have a rowboat, you may have to go by land. Colonel Conant received the signal.

The lights of Somerset lay under the star-filled sky, and the silver moon. The ferries did their work, and 18 miles lay ahead for the red swollen masses. Visit Larkin, heed Devens' warning, and ride fast to avoid peril. Use Hamper's map of the Common but avoid the gallows better than poor Mark. Keep riding toward Washington and Inner Belt, and look for the bronze statue. Next, don't stop at Royal's because he was an adversary.

If you seek amazing Grace, that may be wise. Then head towards Hall's home. Keep bravely traveling on that moonlit silent river road, and then pass an Old Mill. Proceed next to the old spot of Black Horse Tavern. Mr. Lee, Gerry, and Orne of the Safety Committee hid in the field as their foes searched in vain.

Please do not mix this place up with the current Black Horse Tavern Restaurant at 32 Waterfield St. Winchester. That's a great place to eat; owned and run by a very nice retired Winchester Police Officer, and his lovely wife. Winchester is a beautiful town. So swing by and enjoy some dinner at the Pub. If you eat there, please give a polite nod to the Winchester Police, where my distant cousin Daniel proudly sits as their current Chief. What a great man, making his Irish O'Connell family ancestors so proud.

His grandfather and mine were well acquainted back before WW 1, that my grandfather was lucky to survive. He was at Fort Devens Ayer in the US Army, proudly answering Uncle Sam's call. But I think God intervened, and they finally made peace so a single less Muzzey High (Lexington High) graduate wouldn't have to die in those terrible forlorn charges during World War 1.

Then on to Russell's "castle" on the Bay Road, where Cutter was tough as nails. Stop and say hi to Uncle Sam and visit Dallin's Museum if you find time. Now Sam Whittemore's marker stone by Mystic. He was a brave, tough, and stubborn hero who survived the day. Now onto Pierce's Hill; go to the Old Concord Rd. where Menotomy Captain Locke's home still stands.

All of my childhood friends and brothers gave me a lick or more, but our games were fun just the same. Most of us made Adams School and Clarke Junior High proud, especially Mr. Farias, Mr. Conant, and Coach Reed. We grew up on the Arlington-Lexington town line.

Adams School taught us all about biology and sciences. So we tried to learn more on our own, catching worms, grasshoppers, praying mantises, beetles, and spiders in the Great Meadows. My brother Paul had an entire ant colony in a coffee can in our bedroom. In his sleep, he rolled over and knocked the can over. That did not go over too well when ants invaded everyone's beds. There were four of us sleeping barracks-style in two bunk beds. The tiny room really was a den; it had no door or closet. We made the best of it, and never complained but the summers were really hot in that room with no air conditioning or even a fan in the window. Fortunately, we had a small black and white television to watch all the sports games on, and play Pong.

Chris Fuery and I played soccer & ice hockey at Adams (courtesy of Fuery scrapbook)

I have so many treasured memories of us East-Enders, and Hill-toppers fished and had a lot of neighborhood fun near the Old Arlington Res, Sutherland Park, Adams Playground, Courts & Skating Pond, and the Great Meadows with Johnny Bike, Mike Ascolese, Lucky Coyne, Paul Vin, Sefton brothers, Joe, Dools, Babs, Tony Nichols, Gary Collymore, Bobby Aiken, Peter Rommel, Jay & Andy MacAleer, Kelly brothers, John & Chris Oulette, Hedtz, Barry Neal, Jerry Clear, John Walsh, McClaughlin brothers, Bill Ahern, Seneville Family, Eric Steinkrauss, Myers brothers, Collins Family, Chris & Steve Fuery, and so many others. We listened to the Boston & Maine train as it whistled, and chugged on by. Now the Minuteman Bike Path has taken its place, and new families have taken most of our places in these areas.

As I think of all my lifetime friends, I can quietly hear the great 80's song "Time Stand Still" by Rush playing. "…Time stand still… Freeze this moment a lit bit longer. Make each sensation a little bit stronger.

Make each impression a little bit stronger. Freeze this motion a little bit longer. The innocence slips away… Time stand still."

We teenagers hung out on the Hibbert St wall; in the summers of youth, listening to WRKO AM channel on a portable radio playing artists like: Barry Manilow, Peter Frampton, Chicago, Kiss, Elton John, Boston, Fleetwood Mac, etc. It's always fun to be young at heart. From 16 to 60, it all went by so fast.

Me, Babs, Asc, Dools & Joe at our old neighborhood wall Hibbert St by Arnold St. Arlington

We would try to catch butterflies in the purple, and golden meadows at Cataldo's Farm. We caught turtles and fish at "The Secret Pond." We used to play ice hockey there, too. It's now a trail called Cataldo Conservation Land off Bow St. The Cataldo Farm, and its Meadow are sadly gone. Progress made that old farm into South Ridge Road long ago. It's a nice neighborhood just the same. If I had the money, I'd like to move back home to East Lexington but progress and expense has made this seem impossible now.

As young kids we would use strong sticks to move leaves about, looking under logs and rocks searching for our treasures; that being bugs, and salamanders, etc. Mike "Asc" Ascolese lived directly across the street from us at 18 Sylvia St. He and my younger brother Paul would go flipping rocks over, looking for bugs. They found a huge ant hive. Asc said, "Look it's the Queen" pointing. Paul leaned his head close to the hive, and then Asc pushed his head into the nest, and ground it in. So the ants, of course, were all over Paul's face, causing him to retreat. Asc got a good laugh that time. Paul was not too pleased.

Another time, Asc dared Paul to use his bubble gum to trap a Bumblebee in a flower petal. It worked, and the Bumblebee was quite angry. Asc then dared Paul to squeeze the bee inside the flower. Paul took the dare, and immediately screamed in pain, as he got stung in the thumb. His thumb swelled to double its size. Paul learned a painful lesson that time.

Paul got his revenge on Asc though. Paul talked Asc into teasing a yellow jacket hive with him, and about eight yellow jackets flew up Mike's pants. Boy, did he get stung, and ran home to take off his pants. Tough lessons to learn as young teenagers but they learned them well.

My family was particularly poor even for East Lexington standards in the 60's through 80's. What we had, we treasured, and we really did not have much at all. Throughout my life, I collected a bunch of Kennedy, Franklin, and Eisenhower silver coins from when I was a young child. I was very proud of them. Also, when I was in 10th grade, I had a Styx Boston Garden concert ticket. My friend Tony Nichols got me five tickets, and I was supposed to go to the concert with my cute teenage friends: Liza Baumgartner, Stacey Shepard, Lynn Peterson, and Jamie Yales. We were so excited about the Styx concert.

One of my brothers had a girlfriend with a bit of a stealing issue. She carried a big purse; and when she wanted something, she simply put it in her purse with no remorse. She visited my brother at our house in '79 and apparently took my entire coin collection and Styx concert ticket, which she then gave to her younger brother as a gift. Thank heaven she did not steal my stamps, postcards, and patch collections. I still have them. Maybe I will make posters with them some day for fun for all of you to behold.

I was also missing a team-signed Milwaukee Brewer baseball I got from my Aunt Maire Cloherty. Taking the baseball was strange because none of us Boston Red Sox fans liked them anyway. We did begrudgingly respect other good baseball teams though.

Well I was completely stressed out searching for the Styx concert ticket, and she showed up again for my brother. She saw firsthand my anxiety about the loss of my Styx concert ticket. First, she pretended to help me look for the ticket. Then she blamed my poor mother Brigid for cleaning up, and throwing out my Styx ticket. Next, she blamed my brother John's best friend, Steve Kelly, from Oak Street for stealing the Styx ticket.

John "JB" O'Connell "Little Oak" 1969 – 2020 (Old Family photograph)

Steve Kelly and my brother John, called "Little Oak" or "Johnny Bike," were best friends. They spent days on end skating at Adams Pond or playing in the Great Meadows or West Farm fields near the Kelly's Red House on Oak St. The red house is still there on the corner of Oak St and Mass Ave. John and Steve also collected bikes, fixed them up, and sold them. That's why my brother John got the nickname "Johnny Bike" or "JB." I knew Steve Kelly would never steal from my family. He was a loyal friend; his older brother Jimmy was my friend, and his brother Michael was a close friend of my brother, too.

At that point, I realized my brother's girlfriend stole my Styx ticket, and there was nothing I could do but feel heartache because my brother loved her. Love is blind. My brother ignored, denied her faults, and defended her no matter what. It was commendable love but foolhardy loyalty in this case. At some point, that girl left my brother's life, and he moved on in life.

Life sometimes teaches us hard lessons. I still wish I had attended that great Boston Styx concert with my friends but I'm sure her unscrupulous brother enjoyed the Boston Garden ticket; that I paid for, just the same. He likely had no remorse either about the great Styx concert ticket caper, and just played dumb.

Me, Tony Nichols, and Keith Calvin at Depot Square 1980 (LHS 1981 Yearbook photograph)

My 8th-grade pal Tony Nichols lived on Chase Ave. We played full-contact tackle football and softball at Sutherland Park. We played hoops all the time. Those games at Sutherland made us tough warriors and men.

Coach Reed was our Clarke Junior High Football Coach. I loved Coach Reed. He was a great man. Chris Fuery #39 was a Halfback, John Alexander #47 was a Fullback, and John Walsh #50 was the Center. In the fall of '77 all three of them got hurt in our Home game vs. cross-town rival Muzzey Junior High. We end up getting very embarrassed losing 16 to 34. Those Muzzey kids rubbed it in, too.

Barry Neal worked hard and earned every yard & TD (LHS '81 Yearbook)

My close friend Barry Neal played offense & defense in Football and was a star running back all four years. He was Captain of the Lexington High Football team. It was a well-earned honor. Barry was sometimes referred to as a human cannonball!

Sadly, John Walsh and John Alexander died tragically in their early twenties. "Walshy" was a US Marine, and a great friend to all of us. John Alexander was a catcher in baseball, and a great running back. We also lost our friend Brian Adley about 10 years ago to cancer. Brian played baseball and football with us, too. He went with my older brother Joe to Bentley University. I got into Bentley with them but end up going to Northeastern University in Boston.

I played football at LHS. Sophomore year I wore #17 as a Wide Receiver. Junior year Coach made me backup Quarterback, uniform #3. Senior year I was moved off the offense to Defensive Back, #25. So I never impressed anyone on School Football Teams but I learned the whole game, and its strategy well. I would use this knowledge every chance I got playing pickup football which was way more fun to me. There were no whistles, unfair coaches, punishment laps or game delays.

My older brother Joe, and Bobby Aiken also played LHS Football for WW2 US Army Air Corps Veteran Coach Bill Tighe. They both loved to play defense up at Sutherland Park, and they menaced all the other players with their sacks who had no safety equipment on, playing pickup football.

One time, I made a diving off my feet interception. It was a brilliant play. Well, I got up and tried to run for the end zone. That was a big mistake. Bobby Aiken came running in from my left blindside and hit me like a truck, knocking me clear out of bounds into the woods. I was "brave and in the wood (Forrest Fenn)" and held on to the football without fumbling but wished I had stayed down after the interception.

Another time, Joe had intimidated Peter Rommel so badly with his blitz, and hits that Rommel at Center hiked the football like 14 feet in the air. I was the Quarterback and had to scramble backward to try to catch the hike. Joe, of course, blitzed right by Peter and closed rapidly on the ball. So I had two choices: catch the ball and take the hit or allow Joe a fumble recovery touchdown. I elected to take the hit. Joe went airborne with his tackle and struck a defenseless player chest high. He drove me backward 6 or 8 feet. I hit the ground hard but didn't fumble the ball. Joe looked down at me and said, "nice hold." I thought to myself there was no brotherly love or compassion in that hit. Joe just wanted to win by forcing a fumble but he had the wrong quarterback for that. When I say that the right field to center field at Sutherland Park made us tough warriors, it really did. Peter Rommel recently passed, and all of East Lexington shed a tear. He was a great guy, always smiling, and laughing with his friends.

In December '76 or '77, my brother Joe, Bobby Blood, and Ron Blood all worked at Kentucky Fried Chicken on Mass Ave with this Winchester Football player named McConkey. He was bragging about their team's success, and challenged them to play a pickup football game at the really nice varsity Winchester High Football Field. They accepted the challenge, and brought me along. All four of us Lexington guys were wearing our white and blue Lexington High Football practice jerseys when we arrived on that snowy December day.

The Winchester guys brought the Store Manager Ron as their 4th guy. Ron had recently let my brother Joe go from work because business was not good. They elected to receive the football on the kickoff, and Ron was returning the kickoff when my brother Joe absolutely leveled him with a surprise attack. From that point on, we routed the enemy who were completely on the defensive and were forced to surrender. I think I scored 8 touchdowns as a Defensive Back from interceptions on that day. I bet Ron had wished he had not laid Joe off after he took that first hit, and all the other blitzes and hits from Joe, Bobby, and Ronnie Blood that day. We were happy we defeated the enemy, and captured the victory.

Another East Lexington friend, Tony Nichols lived on Chase Ave. He loved rock music. He played the Stones, Ted Nugent, Alice Cooper, Led Zeppelin, and Deep Purple. He wore a t-shirt that said "Disco Sucks." His mom did not like his loud rock music or his t-shirt much. Tony and I went to Providence Center and saw Cheap Trick on their "Dream Police" Tour. Wow, what a show and great song. Tony is an incredible guitarist, and played professionally in "Meliah Rage" and "Mexican Ape Lord" bands. Tony and I are still friends. Sometimes he will call me out of the blue and jump on his Harley Davidson to come see me. What a great friend for about 35 years. He is still playing his electric guitar. Rock on, Tony.

As young children, my brothers and I all ran down Sylvia Street so fast to see Revere & Dawes ride on past every April morning in the late 60's and early 70s.

A young Michael with Harold "Lucky" Coyne (photograph by Marion O'Connell Dolan)

I had a friend named Harold "Lucky" Coyne. Lucky wore #7 as his baseball uniform. He would declare he was "Massachusetts Lucky 7" at an elite Regional Summer Baseball Camp at Cooperstown, NY with players from all nine Northeast states. Lucky confused me because #7 was famous NY Yankee Mickey Mantle's number. But in this work we will give him the benefit of the doubt, and declare Massachusetts "Lucky 7" in my treasure hunts or chases.

Lucky lived at 5 Hibbert St. with his dad, brother Sean, and sister Ann. They had some family stuff going on that was difficult after their parents got divorced. I befriended them all. They used to call me the "4th Coyne." We were always helping Lucky's father Harry fix up their house. He was a proud Charlestown "Townie" and spoke of their bravery fighting the British at Bunker Hill (Breed's Hill). Mr. Coyne really knew Charlestown history well, and I listened closely when he told his tales. He was spot on.

My father had tools, being in the trades. He was not generous with loaning others his tools, and was always afraid he would not get them back. So I would essentially steal them from my Dad and bring them to the Coyne's home. In time, Mr. Coyne would always give me the tools back. He would always say, "Please thank your Father," and I would sneak them back into my Dad's tool collection without him ever noticing they had been borrowed.

I worked a couple of summers at Adams School Playground, taking care of all the East Lexington kids who were dropped off at our camp. I worked with Catherine Woodward LHS Class of '82, then Karen Allen

Class of '81 the next year. Karen was a star softball player, and swimmer at Lexington High.

We ended up becoming close that summer, and dated maybe 4 or 5 weeks. She and I both worked long hours at Adams School and the Town Pools. Karen played summer softball, and I baseball. So we were either playing our games, working, or watching the other play ball. She challenged me to try to be more than I was. Her Dad gave her Red Sox box seats for a game he got from his business, and we went to Fenway. That place is amazing in the summer. The Cathedral of Boston!

Karen wore a cool LHS swimming t-shirt that said "Life in the Fast Lane," a tribute to that great Eagles song always on the radio in the late 70's & early 80's. She swam laps everyday rain or shine. Karen definitely had brown "Bette Davis Eyes" as described in the popular Kim Carnes song. She took off for Syracuse University while I was forced to attend a crappy Community College. I was happy for her but knew she would be better off without me.

We both went our "Separate Ways" like the great Journey song. I think she moved back to Colorado or out west somewhere. I hope she will forgive me for being so frustrated with my lack of opportunities that I was foolishly walking away from a good friend. Sometimes you can be right and wrong at the same time. I should have been kinder to Karen as we went our separate ways. But I was right; she was going to be better off without me, come that Autumn of 1981 on the Syracuse Campus. With Karen gone, I was back to hanging out with my neighborhood friends at age 17.

My friend Harry "Lucky" Coyne was quite the character. He and I went to all kinds of movies like Star Wars and Rocky. We listened to Boston, Meatloaf, Prince and Aerosmith, and watched MTV on a brand new thing called cable TV. We chased girls; sometimes they chased us back, and other times skipping school to meet up with them. Our grades suffered the consequences, and sometimes that meant trouble when you got home and had to answer to your father.

Lucky wasn't shy at all. We were always meeting new girls. He introduced me to this beautiful girl, Jenny Howick, at Belmont High School. She was pretty, smart, and played basketball, too. Like a dummy, I walked away after dating her for about 6 months, thinking I was a couple of years too old for her. I really wasn't. I bet her parents were pleased to get rid of me. She did well in life, and became a Medical Doctor in Maine. Good for her, serving others.

Lucky had a good friend named Sue Zani. She was sweet, kind, and loyal to all her friends. She drove us everywhere. One time she dragged us to a family Labor Day barbecue at Glezen Lane Wayland. Lucky and I did not want to go but Sue forced us. Sue introduced me to her cousin Sharon.

So we played along to help her out. We met her Aunt, Uncle, and cousins. One of them was quite lovely. Within a few days, Lucky called me and said, "Hey, what are you doing?" I said "Studying for college freshman midterms." Lucky said "Study later. That girl Sharon Poisson from Wayland is here now; likes you, and wants to see you now."

So I got dressed quick and Sharon said "Gosh that was fast, let's get in for a ride on the Turnpike in Sue's car." I agreed, and off we just went without a care in the world.

Well, I'm sure I did not get any A's on those college freshman midterms but I had a date with a beautiful brunette. Sometimes fate sends you in the right direction. Sadly, Sue passed early in life. I hope she looks down from her heavenly home, and sees how much she meant to others.

All of my childhood friends, and brothers gave me a lick or more but our games were fun just the same. We kept learning and growing up. Time never stops and does not let you go back. With a strong heart and not much else, I marched on in life.

Let's jump back in time again to 1775. Farmers Porter and Richardson were heading to the Boston market when placed under arrest by the Red Coats in Menotomy. Robbins and Harrington also got caught and were forced to march on with the conquering horde. Wellington fared little better near Sacred Heart Church and Bridal Path.

The Dailey Farm Lexington, MA circa 1861 (photograph by Michael O'Connell)

If you reach the Dailey Farm on Marrett Rd just beyond Follen Rd in the East End, you took the wrong road; turn around and go back to the old Bay Road.

East Lexington treasures: Mary McIver, Bill Dailey, and Father Joe Nangle & Maryelene Dailey

Bill Dailey is East Lexington Irish Catholic royalty and a great friend of mine. We were all so proud when Bill won the White Tricorne Hat (Lexington's greatest citizenship award) on the Lexington Common on Patriot's Day many years back. I cheered so loud for Bill I think all the people in East Lexington heard it. Mrs. Mary McIver was cherished in East Lexington, and a dear friend to my mother Brigid. Father Joe Nangle grew up in East Lexington too and celebrated Mass at the Dailey Farm the day of the above photograph.

Bill went to Muzzey (Lexington) High, Boston College, and Georgetown Law School. Bill's older sister Mary was in my Aunt Marion O'Connell's High School Class. Bill served his nation in the US Navy then as a Lexington Selectman. He is a partner in a prestigious Boston law firm. They once got "the Best of Boston " award. With Bill being a partner there, it was no doubt well earned. His son Bill is a friend of mine as well. He followed in his Father's path. The apple doesn't fall far from the tree on the Dailey Farm.

I tip my hat to both of them, and the rest of the Dailey Clan. Mrs. Maryelene Dailey is a beloved treasure too raising 5 children, and now they have 10 precious grandchildren. The Dailey Clan are a beautiful and special group of people connected to Lexington's Farming History. Just to be clear, there is no treasure on the Dailey Farm so keep going.

Adams, Bowman, and Sgt. Munroe will help show you the way. The owl gets startled as Follen Church's spire rings at midnight as you ride past. As the sun starts to rise in the East, it should be clear that you're on the correct path.

My sisters Mary Ann and Paula never participated in our guy-centered activities because they were busy listening to music, working, or hanging out with their friends. Being a young woman always seemed like so much more work to me. They had to spend too much time taking care of their hair, makeup, clothes, etc. I was so appreciative to simply be a guy, and quickly ride off on my bicycle to go play some sport.

Skating behind Adams School East Lexington by A. Lassell Ripley (author's collection)

Aiden Lassell Ripley lived at his home and art studio at 52 Follen Rd. East Lexington near Sacred Heart Church, Follen Church, and Adams School for over 30 years. He loved Lexington, and was a treasure to the community. He painted a large mural of Lexington's four seasons in the Cary Memorial Library. I love his work, and own a bunch of his very hard to find art prints. Sadly, he died in 1969. He is gone but not forgotten.

We young men in East Lexington all skated at Adam's Pond, chased butterflies in the Great Meadows, turtle hunted, played football, hoop, or street hockey as Sylvia, Hibbert, Taft, and Sutherland neighbors watched our youth and vigor. You can take the man out of the boy but you can't take the boy out of the man. Many things you loved or enjoyed; as a youth, are still valued when you are much older.

Us young teenagers harnessed the energy of Gerry Rafferty's "Baker Street," Garry Wright's "Dreamweaver," and "Afternoon Delight" by Starland Vocal Band. We liked the girls by 4th through 8th grade, but they never seemed much interested in our antics at that age. Once in a while, they would spend time with us at school dances.

They were all so very pretty with gorgeous hair, ribbons, makeup, and perfume. Us guys had much to learn about the fairer gender. I basically just stuck to playing sports and avoided the game of love at this point in life. Little did I know; the challenges that lay ahead, where angels wisely would fear to tread.

When I was in 5th & 6th grade, Mark "Hedtz" Hedtler and I were best friends. We walked home on a winter day and decided to throw snowballs at passing cars on Mass Ave near Oak St by Shimansky's Garage. Hedtz fired an ice ball, and smashed the driver's side window of a passing tow truck. Boy, did we run for it. Hedtz took off up Oak Street Hill towards his house near Carville Ave.

I ran up Oak St then took the first left toward Hilltop, then a sudden right across the Bowker Conservation land trail overlooking Mass Ave heading east for Bowker St, then took folks backyards to Charles St, Cherry St, across Taft Ave then over the fence to my parents' house on Sylvia Street.

Thank heaven, I knew that "Bowker Wood" well from when Kevin Dooley and I used to play pretend Minutemen soldiers, firing downhill with our stick muskets at the passing British troops. We were "brave and in the wood" as Forrest Fenn noted. Kevin and I always beat the British. Both of us being of Irish descent, we believed it was our duty.

Kevin's Mother Dorothy (Foley) Dooley grew up in Woburn. She was a great lady to us kids. She is now resting in peace for all time with her husband James at Saint Mary's Cemetery in Tewksbury, near Captain Trull's old home site (current Trull Brook Golf Course), not a far drive from my home in Andover. I always think of her, and her husband Jim when I pass by. They were both very kind to me as I child; and it meant a lot back then, perhaps more then they realized.

I was a little out of breath from the not quite a mile full-speed run to safety after the tow truck incident. Thank heaven Hedtz and I never got caught. My Dad would have whipped me once again with his leather belt for such an offense. Also, we did not have the money to pay for that tow truck window. With the oil embargo going on and my Dad always laid off from his construction work; as a Union Plumber and Pipe Fitter, the 70's and 80's were always tough times for our family. Six children was a very large family with little income to support them. We were really poor. It was very difficult.

Our neighbor, poor Old Helen, should have ducked; she took a snowball directly in the face after my older brother Joe baited me. Not my finest moment as she hollered, "Michael, you damn bastard." Her husband Bill hollered like hell at me too, and I deserved it. I should have avoided that snowball fight with my brother Joe, and stuck to sledding "the Piggy" at West Farm on my really fast Yankee Clipper sled that I got from Santa Claus. It was perhaps the greatest present I ever got.

My brother Joe and I walked up Taft Ave to Baker Ave, then to Oak Street with our sleds. Joe had a nice red plastic sled. He went and got his Oak St friend Mike Seneville, and I went across the street and got Mark "Hedtz" Hedtler.

Mark Hedtler circa 1981 old photo (courtesy of Chris Fuery)

My friend Hedtz tried out my Yankee Clipper at the "Piggy" in 6th grade. In 1975, Hedtz rode it far too fast heading toward the gap in the stonewalls and lost control. Hedtz went sailing in the air, and then hit the sole tree in the center of the valley on the farm slope head-on. Oh no, he split his forehead open at impact, and was bleeding everywhere. That was the end of our fun.

I had to quickly get Hedtz back out of farmer Old Man West's gates to his 62 Oak Street home to his Mom. Mark was hurt bad. Hedtz's stepfather was not nice at all. He seemed mean to me, and Hedtz all the time. Joe took care of my Yankee Clipper while we got Hedtz home. Joe was too smart to go to the house, though, and kept walking toward Sylvia Street. I was going to be in big trouble here.

Mark's mother treasured him, so of course, she was mad as hell that he got hurt badly on my sled. I always used old wax candles on my sled's metal tracks before I took it out. It really flew. It was my greatest treasure back then, and I was the glory of the "Piggy" Hill. After the Mark Hedtler crash, I wisely did not let others ride her again. The Yankee Clipper was mine, and mine alone.

My son Corey puts my old sled in our Christmas display every year (photo by author)

I still have my Yankee Clipper sled. We display it every December as part of our outside Christmas decorations. I have fond memories of sledding faster down the Piggy Hill than any other kid in East Lexington. The Piggy is on the beautiful West Farm, now conservation land, made famous by Ripley's beautiful artwork on the cover of a book about him.

"February" view across Wilson Farm by A. Lassell Ripley (Author's collection)

Hedtz was a star basketball player, but he couldn't hit a baseball or take a good hit in football. The girls all loved him because he was tall, good-looking, athletic, and charming. Us guys loved Hedtz but didn't appreciate him stealing all of the hearts of the beautiful girls. Sadly, Mark died of a sudden stroke a few years back. The basketball courts at Adam's Playground should be named of LHS Basketball Captain Mark "Hedtz" Hedtler for he was the King of the Courts in Lexington. His Basketball Coach Bob Farias is there in spirit too telling us kids how to shoot the basketball with a proper backspin, dribble and drive on the net.

Chris Fuery, Barry Neal, and I were all there and spoke at Mark's graveside service. Chris grew up on the corner of Mass Ave and Pleasant St (The Old Brown Farm Historic Home) and his Grandfather owned Wilson's Farm. Barry grew up on Spencer St. Kevin Dooley grew up on Taft Ave.

Old Fashioned Wilson's Paper Bag (courtesy of Chris Fuery Scrapbook)

Dools, Barry, Chris, and Hedtz were all great athletes. They always earned the Presidential Physical Fitness award and patches. I had no flexibility, so I never got it once. They were always better athletes than me. I was younger too and always chasing behind them. But just being around them always made me a better athlete as a youth.

I pray Mark and our 6th-grade Adams School teacher, Coach Bob Farias; play hoop and golf together in heaven. Their remains are close together at Westview Cemetery. When I get a chance to visit, I always pray for both of them.

My brother Paul Vincent and I used to play hoops with Scott Figenbaum in his Charles Street driveway. Paul was always happy, smiling, laughing, and doing his thing as a young man or kid. Scott is gone now; he left his family way too soon. My youngest brother John was a close friend of Kirt Figenbaum for all of his life. Steve Kelly and Kirt tried their best to help my brother John. He sadly chose not to listen to them or anyone else, but I thank them for trying to help John.

My father always had these long, awful jobs or tasks in mind for us in the summer or on weekends. We all would rather be any other place than working our tails off beside him for a free glass of tap water. My Dad was a spectacularly generous soul. Laugh out loud.

So my younger brother Paul would always wisely agree to help to avoid some fight with our Dad. He would get dressed, then go in the backyard, and jump the fence. He would laugh, and take off to Sean Hosford's house on Taft Ave. I did not blame Paul that much. The jobs were always time-consuming, boring, dirty, and awful hard work.

Of course, that meant twice as much work for me but Paul never thought of others that much as a youth. My Dad called Paul the "Fence Hopper." It was a well-earned title. For much of his teenage years, Paul always jumped the fence, and left the work mostly for me. My father never seemed surprised when Paul took off, and he never got in trouble for it either. I guess Paul had the luck of the Irish.

Paul moved about an hour west of our Parents' home on Sylvia St Lexington. He is married with four grown children. Paul ended up being a very hard worker. He is always working two jobs to support his family. He is still good friends with Sean Hosford.

Bobby Orr made the score, and Carlton "Pudge" Fisk did his immortal leap and dance around the bases. It was Larry Bird vs. Julius "Dr. J" Erving, Magic Johnson, or Michael Jordan. We young lads cheered with thunder as the Goodyear blimp flew overhead yonder toward and then later back from Fenway's Green Monster when Cincinnati came to town for the World Series in 1975. Sadly, the Sox didn't break the curse of the Babe Ruth trade that year.

My father, Joseph, loved John Wayne and Clint Eastwood movies. The Outlaw Josey Wales was one of our favorites. He had some neat antique pistols and black powder rifles in his collection. They did not normally fire but collected dust really well. Sometimes my Dad would load his replica pistol or muskets and upset the neighbors with a loud blast from our backyard porch.

The neighbors often called the police about my Dad's antics. They did not appreciate his 10 PM humor much on those hot summer nights when everyone's windows were open. We would all take cover, and the police cruiser would just drive on by. They knew it was my Dad but the drive by served to end the problem for the night every time.

Our family and friends often walked around or fished at the Old Arlington Res with my youngest brother John "Johnny Bike." We could see the Arlington Res from our kitchen window on Sylvia St. As a young child, I swung peacefully on the swing set my Dad built in the backyard. I would look up at those big beautiful cumulus clouds and hum to myself, "What a Wonderful World" (Louis Armstrong).

My Dad Joe, Mom Brigid, Aunt Eileen, Uncle Charlie, Grandma, Aunts Marion & Peggy & Lynn

Last time I was on the Sylvia St, I looked up at the majestic cumulus clouds and brilliant blue skies and thought of my mother Brigid, father Joseph, and brother John. I prayed for their souls and asked John to send me a sign. Instantly, the clouds formed a giant smile in the beautiful blue sky but it passed by too quickly; like my brother's spirit and smile, for me to photograph it. When I got home, I told my wife about the clouds, and she thought it was John sending a sign, too. I believe their souls must all be happy in heaven with all our ancestors. May God bless them.

My father and I talked about all great battles and military leaders for what seemed like 50 years. My Dad especially loved the stories about the American Revolution and the US Civil War. When we had the chance, we went to some of those places. He collected all sorts of Civil War guns, WW1 helmets, and Revolutionary War memorabilia. I inherited his Savage Civil War pistol. I also love history and collecting; it must be a family trait.

My Aunts Peggy and Maire Cloherty at my Parent's Wedding reception at St Brigid's Hall

My beautiful Irish Aunts Maire Cloherty, and Susan Doherty helped feed and care for us kids on half-days from school on Thursday afternoons. My grandmother was also a great help. Without them, Brigid (Bridie) and Joe would have been all done. Susan died in '73, and I have visited her Westview Cemetery grave often over the last 51 years. Gone but not forgotten, God bless all our ancestors' souls.

In '69, my beautiful Irish mother Brigid brought her six children back home. I have loved Ireland ever since. My Mom had a heart of gold. She died far too young from diabetes at 59. We all wept bitter tears, wishing we had done more for our Mom. She now rests in Westview Cemetery by the Bedford line with so many dear loved ones of mine.

My Aunt Maire Cloherty brought me back to my Grandparent's Farm in Ireland in '72. She once said to me "Michael your heart is free, have the courage to follow it." She was always one of the strongest positive influences in my life, like a Mother. She is now 90, and still stubbornly refuses to live with us. She has always chosen to live life her way.

My Aunt Ann Beatty's London daughter Jackie Johnstone and her husband Mark now own and care for our Grandparent's cottage and farmland. That gorgeous place right by the ocean has been in the Cloherty Family for about 800 years. I hope it keeps going on forevermore. I really do love that beautiful part of Ireland.

My Aunt Maire said the Walsh's and Cloherty's were always very smart. My cousin Michael Cloherty Jr. proved her point. He wrote a great Malden history book called Abel Bodied. I own an author-signed first edition of this book. He is a pretty good writer, so I thought I would try to capture people's imagination with my two books.

On a side note, my Grandmother Brigid Walsh was from Carna. She is a great aunt of former Boston Mayor Marty Walsh. So I have at least one famous cousin. No matter if you like his politics or not, Marty Walsh comes from great Irish stock! That's really not a bad thing at all in a city that always honors the Celtics.

If you have gotten hungry, please stop by Wilson's Farm; say hi to my good friend Scott Wilson, LHS class of 1980, former great 1st baseman, and grab a quick bite to eat for lunch. Although, those family farms going back to the 1800's are absolutely wonderful, I did not hide any treasure at Wilson's Farm.

West Farm abutting Wilson's Farm goes back to at least the 1800's as well. I think the Piggy is where they raised pigs on that West Farm long ago. Scott's mom Lynne lives there now. She has always been loved by all, and is an East Lexington treasure.

When Babe Ruth and Lefty Gomez played for the Boston Braves they used to hang out in East Lexington. Lefty Gomez lived on Oak St near West Farm, and they are rumored to have played catch and drank some beer on West Farm. Where Arlex Oil currently is at 275 Mass Ave Lexington used to be a popular place where folks ate and hung around. Babe Ruth; and Lefty Gomez, likely ate there back in the day.

I love Wilson Farm and go there all the time for flowers, apple pie, and all kinds of yummy, healthy food. I often bring their flowers or crumb cakes to my Aunt Maire in Malden Center or home to my wife and youngest son.

A new generation has taken our place on the Liberty Heights hill and in East Lexington. I met this great Bowman Elementary School youth, Billy. I call him "Billy the Kid." Billy did not get to attend Adams Elementary School because it closed long ago; and is now the private Waldorf School of Lexington but the Town still owns the soccer fields, tennis courts, basketball court, and Adams Skating Pond behind the building. The Town of Arlington owns the Great Meadows behind the old train tracks now called the Minuteman Bikeway. Lexington was forced by the State many years ago to sell Arlington those Great Meadows to protect their Old Arlington Reservoir water supply.

Billy's mom, Catherine, is a Lexington "Townie" and grew up on Hancock St., not far from the historic Hancock-Clarke House, which is definitely worth a visit. Billy's dad, Bill, is a great guy, too. I even got to know Billy's grandparents who still live in their Hancock Street home. They regularly walk downtown, and drive their beloved Grandson Billy all over the place.

So all of my children are over 18, and my wife Laurel gives away much of their old toys, etc., to clean and organize our home. So I keep an eye out for stuff that "Billy the Kid" may like or use for a while. With his parents' permission, I gave him an 1800's Old West Sheriff's badge from my collection. His Mom told me he then dressed up as a Police Officer for Halloween. I love that because I also trick-or-treated Taft Ave, Baker Ave, Peacock Farm Rd, and the whole area as a child. Good for Billy. That's the spirit.

Another time, I left Billy a giant bug collection kit and a wooden walking staff my son Ryan made in Cub Scouts. So Billy was all set to take a bug hunting expedition in the Sutherland Woods with his Dad. I didn't want to get in BIG trouble with his mom, so I left Billy a note in his bug-catching gear to please set the bugs free before going into his parent's or Grandparent's homes.

Catherine and Bill have a great sense of humor. When I see them around town, I always taunt them a bit, saying Billy needs Dunkin' Donuts, Ice Cream, or Wilson Farm's cider donuts and chocolate milk. His parents try to keep him off the sugar but Billy and I have a good laugh in the process. I'm pretty sure though that I helped "Billy the Kid" get some ice cream or donuts over the years. "Billy the Kid" promised to take care of the Old Arlington Reservoir, Adams Playground, Sutherland Woods, Sutherland Park, and the Piggy for me. I appreciate that because my brothers, our friends, and I spent numerous hours of our childhood in all these spots.

I made sure to tell Billy and his parents about how my friend sled head-on into that tree, split his head open, and likely had a concussion. They plan to sled safely around that tree in the middle of the sledding hill at the "Piggy" in the winter.

Clarke Junior High School Yearbook Yesterday 1976 – 1977 (Author's Collection)

Not too far in the future, Billy will head off to Clarke Middle School, where my wife and I attended and all our siblings, too. To his mother's chagrin, I taught Billy the phrase "Clarke rules, Diamond drools." She always defends Diamond Middle School having attended there, and that is fair enough.

William Diamond's drum at Lexington April 19, 1775 (courtesy of Lexington Historical Society)

Diamond is a great school named after William Diamond, who was the drummer on Lexington Common on April 19, 1775. William Diamond's drum is still preserved by the Lexington Historical Society. I played a lot of baseball and football on the Diamond fields. I met my future wife there for the very first time on their soccer fields when we were coaching youth soccer. I have so many great memories at Diamond Junior High (now Middle School).

Catherine is a good sport. I know East Lexington is safe in her family's care, and I can smile because Billy and his friends are doing just as me, my brothers, and East Lexington friends did back in the 60's, 70's, and 80's. I have great faith that "Billy the Kid" will do really well at Lexington High School, and then head off to a great college or university. Go, Billy; seek out your dreams, and continue to make your parents and grandparents proud.

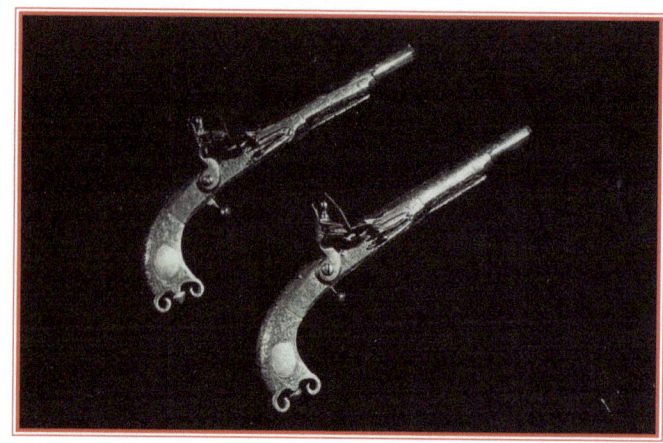

Crosbie pistols were in Lexington, Lincoln and Concord 4/19/75 (Lexington Historical Society)

From the Adams School Playgrounds, keep heading west. Perhaps then plan a stop to see British-Irish Captain William Crosbie's 38th Regiment of Foot (circa April 19, 1775) steel Murdoch pistols that were once falsely attributed to British Major John Pitcairn. The pistols now reside at their new red home. General Percy may help you find your way. Then continue on your journey of exploration.

My childhood; then our children's, passed by so fast. As a young child, I attended Kindergarten at the Gray Nun's Academy on Pelham Rd. My older siblings went to the Gray Nuns Academy, too. In the winter, after school my Dad would let us go sledding in the park on Mass Ave across from Pelham Rd. For a young child, that was a great after school activity. There were always lots of children sledding there.

In later years at this park, we watched General Percy's Reenactors firing their muskets or cannon while the swarm of angry Minutemen from many communities gave pursuit. My father Joseph always loved going to this event every April, regardless of the weather. He particularly enjoyed the cannon fire. New England can have cold and damp Aprils but it's definitely a great Retreat Battle to watch the muskets fire; and the cannon roar, if the weather is favorable. If not, come back and enjoy it a future year.

His Majesty's 10th Regiment of Foot wants you to join (Courtesy of www.redcoat.org)

The 10th Regiment passed by here heading west before sunrise. They were ordered by General Gage to find stolen brass cannon, powder, shot, other implements of war, and arms.

Retired Lexington Police Officer Peter "Rock" Scopa (Scopa Family photograph)

When you reach the Old Bay Rd (Mass Ave at Waltham St), please remember Center Officer Peter "Rock" Scopa. He grew up on Bow St in East Lexington, later moved to Reed St. His sister Rose owned Bellino's Donuts with her husband Veto. Lexington Firefighter Mark Bellino is their son, and he has spent much of his life in the East Lexington Fire Station. Officer Peter Scopa likely saw more Lexington Patriot's Day parades, and reenactments then any officer ever.

Rock was a fixture in Lexington Center. Us teenagers never dared to jaywalk or cause trouble with him on the foot beat in Lexington Center. I was friendly with his children Carolyn, Peter John, and Leann. The Rock and I became good friends. We enjoyed many good laughs over the years. He retired to the Lakes Region of New Hampshire.

Peter John Scopa, and I played pickup hoop and football together growing up. We hung out a lot with Lexington or surrounding Towns friends: Liz Malin, Lauren Forbes, Tracy Sutherland, Stacey Harrington, Ariadne Sokolov, Eric Crosby, Leann Scopa, Judy Tighe, Jackie Selway, Scott Figenbaum, Sue Porter, Genevieve Parent, Laura Eaton, Sharon MacKay, Mike O'Keefe, Lucky Coyne, Sue Zani, Sharon Poisson, Tina Bianci, Kim Wooters, Laurine Marino, Dolores Clark, Dan Puffer, Amy Puffer, Keith Girouard, and many others. They were all nice. We all had a lot of fun and laughed together. They were all great teenage friends.

Peter John tried to get me to date his beautiful sister Leann but I was too afraid and respectful of the Rock to consider such a bold move. Peter now lives in the family home on Reed St raising his own family.

When you reach Lexington Center, if your feet get sore from hiking or walking, stop in Michelson's Shoes, established in 1919. Ask for my friends Eric or Jerry Michelson. They graduated from Lexington High in the 80's, later took over the family business when their father Dick sadly passed. Eric used to live at the Muzzey High Condos. He could easily walk back, and forth to work. Jerry is a "Townie" and lives near the Maple St Bridge over the Minuteman Bikeway.

Dick Michelson proudly won the White Tricorne hat on Patriot's Day in '75 or '76 when America was celebrating its Bicentennial. Eric or Jerry will happily help you get some new sneakers to end the blisters because the search goes on and on for *Lady Liberty's* treasure. Lexington and Concord are currently planning for April 19, 2025 250 years after the first fights for liberty.

Lexington Town Hall Display Board (photograph by Michael O'Connell)

My brother Joe, and I were standing right across from the Captain Parker Statue when President Ford spoke there in 1975. We got to shake President Gerald Ford's hand. At the end of the ceremony; we ran across the street, and Joe plucked some leaves off the wreath President Ford had placed there. One of the old guys from the Celebration's Committee was not too pleased, and he quickly slapped Joe's hand. Joe was 12 at the time and ran off. I still have some of those Bicentennial stamps on letters that we mailed home under that historic A. Lassell Ripley art mural inside the Lexington Post Office.

Lexington Common April 19, 1775 by Don Troiani National Guard Series (Public Domain)

Poor Porter tried to run and was shot down by an angry Officer's pistol. The others never had much of a chance to follow the order to disperse. The echo of the Officer's pistol that killed Porter likely caused the sympathetic fire by his compatriots. This tragedy caused the shot heard round the world and a second massacre that led to war. William Barnes Wollen's art depicts the scene. He traveled from England for posterity's sake. Every "Townie" knows in their hearts that the treacherous foes fired first as the Minutemen and Militia tried to flee to avoid them. Revolutionary War Historical Artist Amos Doolittle thought so as well. So did Patriot Thomas Fessenden in his sworn statement.

Perhaps go into the truly great Lexington Visitor's Center. Look at all the cool displays, and ask for directions to the Minuteman National Park Visitor's Center on the Lexington-Lincoln Line. Take a close look at the USS Lexington art prints housed there. I proudly collected them, got them signed by veterans who served on those ships on Patriot's Day, and donated them as a proud son of Lexington to the town for display. I think it's really cool that so many historic US Navy ships were named in honor of our town. My longtime friends Dawn McKenna and Eric Michelson made certain they were displayed in a place of honor in our new Visitor's Center. Like many who love the town, I am a member of the Lexington Historical Society and a permanent member of the Friends of Minuteman National Park (Lexington, Lincoln, and Concord), and so is my youngest son Corey.

LEXINGTON GREEN.

BOSTON & MAINE SERIES.

Old image of Lexington Green with the Hancock Cannon? (Author's postcard collection)

My father told me a Lexington classic tale that the above 6 pound cannon was stolen by the Concord High School students due to Town rivalry over who fired the first shot. He said the gun was taken overnight and moved to Concord for their home Thanksgiving Football game vs their annual rival Lexington in the 1940's. He said the Town of Lexington sent their police or DPW to get their cannon back and cemented it in front of Muzzey High School. That certainly sounds like a tall tale to me.

Another Old Timer from Lexington said the above picture is of the original "Hancock" Cannon, and the Massachusetts State Police took it from Lexington Green on orders of their Governor to preserve it, and that it now resides in the National Park Liberty St. Concord. The second version may be possible but I have found no proof of it, yet.

Now pass the shadow of the gun there night and day; then drawing nigh up over Concord Hill where my friends David Bresnihan, Rick & Brian Ham, and Paul Jenkins all grew up. Soon enough you will pass Hartwell's brilliant but terrible sight. Watch out for Major Mitchell of the 5th Regiment. He may point his pistol to stop your advance. The first wounds were given nearby. John Daniels completed a drawing about this in 1903.

Nelson was the first to be wounded in this affair. A saber cut to the head sent the message. Captain William Smith soon spread the alarm. A nest of British officers captured a lone rider but the other two got away. A. Lassell Ripley was here; then well after him so was Cortney Skinner to study and paint this interesting event. They both did their best but I think Skinner's art version is more accurate.

Perhaps see the 2019 movie *Little Women* starring Emma Watson. It's based upon a famous book written nearby. That was one of my wife Laurel's favorite books as a young woman, and we saw that movie together. It was well done and filmed in several nearby places.

Wright Tavern circa 1673 Concord Center (photograph by Michael O'Connell)

So go off to Prescott's home marker among the stone wall as fast as you may safely go, then on to Wright's place, for you must have a thirst by now to quench. Doolittle noted that Smith, and Pitcairn climbed the Old Burial Ground to get a better view, but the dead were in no position to complain.

Dr. Prescott rode through Lincoln, Concord, East Acton, Acton Center, then to Minuteman Simon Hunt's Farm (now Liberty Tree Farm), and up the road to Stowe to spread the alarm. Prescott's warning assured enough Provincial Militia were present at North Bridge to engage the British in Concord. Dr. Samuel Prescott had asked his brother Abel to spread the alarm as well. Abel Prescott's truly important ride went from the area by the First Parish & Wright Tavern Concord to First Parish Sudbury Center, and then he further alerted Framingham. This led to battle later in the day.

Abel Prescott on his April 19, 1775 ride to First Parish Sudbury (by Monica Vachula PRR 2003)

History seems to have forgotten Abel Prescott's ride that was majorly important to the Provincial Militia victory near the Bloody Angle in Lincoln. Abel Prescott was later shot; on his return ride to town by the British Troops somewhere between the South Bridge area, and Concord Center when he refused to surrender.

Abel Prescott rode off with his wound, and his brother Dr. Prescott later treated him. Even though his brother was a skilled Medical Doctor; Abel's wound never healed properly, infection set in, and the mortal wound took his life in August 1775. Abel was only 24 or 25 and is presumed buried at an unmarked grave in an unknown spot at Concord. Likely Abel is in the Old Burial Ground since their family home was so close to there on the Lexington Road. Perhaps the old wooden cross simply rotted away over time. Concord resident Abel Prescott gave his life for his young nation, and should never be forgotten.

On Lexington Road, Lincoln marched east. They soon observed the conquering foe as their bayonets glittered in the sun upon their purposeful march, and wisely listened to their Captain William Smith and went pouring back across Concord Center to rally with the others upon the Punkatasset Hill.

One of the original North Church lanterns is at the Concord Museum (Author's collection)

Don't make Colonel Barrett angry until you cross the river, or Punkatasset's bee swarm will soon be on you. Harry Jaecks and Don Troiani did some of their best artworks here. The foe came on searching for brass cannon "6-pounders" and supplies that were long gone moved to Acton, Groton or Stow. 3 to 8 Groton Militia Men took the initiative and went to Concord even though the Groton Town Meeting had voted to wait until further orders before acting. Carlisle (then part of Concord and Billerica), and Westford responded as well.

Longfellow had it wrong, but his poetry was just embellished a bit. His close friends Hawthorne, Thoreau, Emerson, French, and Alcott likely took note. They all now lie together in the Sleepy Hollow.

General Henry Hunt standing by tent entrance right of Major General Meade (Public Domain)

MICHAEL CLOHERTY O'CONNELL

Henry Hunt's fame at Malvern Hill, Sharpsburg, and Gettysburg was well earned. He fought with honor with McClellan, Warren, Slocum, Meade, Hancock, Chamberlain, Meagher, and Grant. They melted Hunt's mighty Union guns just the same for an altogether different contest for French's immortal fame. French made Captain Isaac Davis immortal with his great work. Even President Grant came to look upon it in 1875.

Hunt paid with blood for those guns. Gettysburg was quite the fight. Union General Hunt must have had quite the view. Hunt gazed across to his foe's cannon fire. Confederate General Porter Alexander soon learned he was outsmarted and outgunned. Somewhere between General Hunt and General Slocum, Major General Meade found his treasure in their grit, men or by their cannon. I recently acquired General Hunt and General Slocum's autographs on old documents. Between the two of them, what a treasure.

Hancock the Superb and his Fighting Irish Brigade knocked back Generals Lee, Longstreet, and Pickett's charge. Custer did well charging at Hampton across the East Field, too. So Longstreet, Stuart and Lee were forced to retreat back across Marsh Creek toward Fairfield then to Falling Waters. Gettysburg was their last march north.

Vermont's Greatest Civil War hero Major William Wells & 1st VT cavalry (photo by author)

Chamberlain proudly earned a Medal of Honor for his gallant bayonet charge on this great battlefield at Little Roundtop. Major William Wells earned a Medal of Honor at Gettysburg also with his First Vermont Cavalry during Farnsworth's charge.

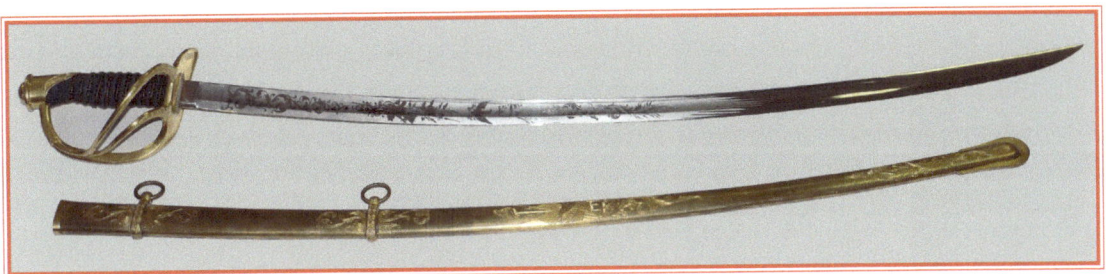

1st VT Cavalry Captain George B. Conger's sword (courtesy of St Albans Museum)

I also have signed documents from Generals William Wells and Joshua Chamberlain. Other great treasures! Captain George B. Conger also served on the First Vermont Cavalry. Captain Conger was home on injury leave then led the pursuit of CSA Lt Bennett Young's irregular Cavalry at St Albans Vermont in October 1864 into Canada. Please visit the St Albans Museum 9 Church St to learn all about their city's history.

Union Major General John Reynolds led First Corps to Gettysburg (Public Domain photo)

History can be really sad, at times. Major General John Reynolds was from Lancaster, Pennsylvania. After General Burnside's defeat at Fredericksburg and the Mud March disaster, Lincoln desired a new Army of the Potomac Commander. On June 3, 1863, President Lincoln offered Major General John Reynolds command of the Army of the Potomac. Unfortunately General Reynolds had concerns about the War Department Generals Halleck; and Stanton in Washington D.C. causing too much negative interference with the Army, so he declined the command offer. Lincoln then turned to another more Junior Pennsylvanian Officer, General George Meade, and made him Commander of the Army of the Potomac. Fate can be fickle. John Reynolds might have survived the Civil War had he accepted command of the Army of the Potomac, as George Meade survived the war. Lincoln was smart to consider Pennsylvania men to command the army of the Potomac because they knew the ground best.

General Meade placed his close friend General John Reynolds in charge of the 1st, 3rd, and 11th Corps. As the left wing of the Army of the Potomac, Meade sent Reynolds ahead towards Robert E. Lee's Army of Northern Virginia. On July 1, 1863, Reynolds led the 1st Corps across Sauches Bridge in Gettysburg with the 11th & 3rd Corps following behind.

Fighting for Time (General Buford) by Don Stivers (Courtesy of donstivers.com)

Reynolds could hear the sounds of battle and saw civilians fleeing south on the Emmitsburg Road in Gettysburg. He hurried to the Lutheran Seminary and found Union Cavalry General John Buford and his troopers fighting off CSA General Harry Heth of General A.P. Hill's Corps. Buford was delaying the Confederates from seizing the high ground from Cemetery Hill to the two Roundtop Mountains beyond the Town of Gettysburg.

From the cupola of the Lutheran Seminary, Reynolds called up to Buford, "What's the matter, John?" Buford replied, "There's the devil to pay." Recognizing the strategic defensive ground, Reynolds sent a message to General George Meade: "I will fight the enemy inch by inch, and if driven into town I will barricade the streets and hold him back as long as possible."

Generals John Buford & John Reynolds July 1, 1863 (Gettysburg National Park Public Image)

Reynolds and Buford initiated a battle that would last three days. Reynolds positioned his arriving units, and as the 2nd Wisconsin rushed past, he shouted, "Forward men, forward, for God's sake, and drive those fellows out of the woods."

The fall of General Reynolds at Gettysburg by Alfred Waud (Public Domain)

During the heavy fighting, Reynolds was about 75 yards away from the Confederates by Herbst Woods, was likely struck and killed by a 7th Tennessee Regiment's volley, making him the highest-ranking Union officer killed in battle during the Civil War. He was buried in his nearby hometown of Lancaster, Pennsylvania. So truly sad, all of America wept for General Reynolds. President Abraham Lincoln noted that Major General John Reynolds, and others gave "the last full measure of devotion" for their nation. General Reynolds was the highest-ranking Union General killed during the US Civil War. Both sides respected him, and felt the loss.

Without Major General Reynolds' leadership, the Union defense faltered. CSA Lt. Generals A.P. Hill and Richard Ewell soon swept the field. General Robert E. Lee won the first day and climbed to the top of the Lutheran Seminary cupola. However, Lee made a critical error by giving General Ewell discretionary orders, assuming he would take Cemetery Hill, and the Roundtops. Lee's reliance on the aggressive actions of the late Lt. General Stonewall Jackson; who had died from friendly fire at Chancellorsville, proved misguided. Generals Ewell and Early were not equals to General Jackson. Despite the setbacks, fate favored Union Major General George Meade at Gettysburg.

My friend Andy Brown, Bowdoin College alum, admires General Joshua Chamberlain. I gifted him a Don Troiani print of Chamberlain's famous charge down Little Roundtop at Gettysburg. Chamberlain was born in Brewer, Maine and taught at Bowdoin College. He is commemorated with sculptures in his home state, and a nearby museum at 226 Maine St. Brunswick, Maine. While my children sadly didn't attend Bowdoin, it's a beautiful campus worth visiting, especially for young students.

Andy and I still talk regularly, and plan to visit Gettysburg again. We want to see the direction Reynolds led his Union Corps from Fairfield across Sauches Bridge, to Lutheran Seminary and Herbst Wood. We also want to visit where Farnsworth and Chamberlain made their famous charges. I also want to see the Irish Brigade's famous positions July 1 - 3, 1863 on the Battlefield. Lastly, we want to pay our heartfelt respects at General John Fulton Reynolds grave in Lancaster, Pennsylvania to pray for his great soul.

I've been to Gettysburg many times. It's a solemn yet remarkable place to visit with family, and friends. One can see where soldiers gave their "last full measure of devotion," as Lincoln so eloquently said in his Gettysburg address. Freedom is not free; we must fight to preserve it. For more detailed information about The Battle of Gettysburg, I recommend "They Met at Gettysburg" by US Army Retired Colonel Edward Stackpole.

General Lee won the first day at Gettysburg but lost at Little Roundtop, and many soldiers from both armies died on the second day. On the third day, Lee ordered Lt. General James Longstreet to send Generals Pickett, Pettigrew, and Trimble across a mile of open field. During Pickett's charge, the brave CSA General Lewis Armistead reached the Bloody Angle but was mortally wounded, while his friend Union General Winfield Hancock was also injured. Armistead died two days later in a Union Field Hospital. Before his death, he had entrusted his personal effects to General Hancock's wife. Generals Reynolds, Armistead and Hancock were close friends.

CSA General Lewis Armistead with Union Capt. Henry Bingham (Public Domain)

Hancock was deeply saddened at losing his dear friends in the Battle of Gettysburg. He praised Armistead's bravery in his eulogy and wrote a letter to Armistead's family, describing him as "one of the bravest and most gallant soldiers I have ever known." General Armistead is buried next to his uncle, Lt. Colonel George Armistead, at Old St. Paul's Cemetery in Baltimore. The Star-Spangled Banner, inspired by Fort McHenry's defense, forever marks the Armistead Family's great American legacy.

President Lincoln & General McClellan at Antietam 1862 (Alexander Gardner Public Domain)

Gettysburg is a great town to visit, and has it's own college. There was a recent movie filmed there, and released in 2023 called *A Gettysburg Christmas*. The town embraced it. Now every first weekend of December they run a neat Christmas and Holiday Festival. If folks wish to see the movie, it plays at Seminary Ridge inside Valentine Hall. You can get information about movie reservations at: www.agettysburgchristmasfestival.com .

When walking the Gettysburg Battlefield, one can sense the immense valor and tragedy. Estimated casualties were 23,049 Union and 28,063 Confederate. Union General George Meade's victory at Gettysburg was hard-fought. CSA General Robert E. Lee retreated from Gettysburg on July 4th riding along with Longstreet's First Corps heading back over the Marsh Creek Bridge toward Fairfield then to Williamsport and Falling Waters, Maryland to cross the Potomac River back to the safety, and supplies of Northern Virginia. President Lincoln, frustrated by Lee's escape, recognized the importance of never forgetting the sacrifices made in his famous Gettysburg Address.

This sentiment applies to all military veterans. President John F. Kennedy during his 1961 Inaugural address said: "Ask not what your country can do for you, ask what you can do for your country." Kennedy, a student of history who served in the US Navy on PT 109 in WWII, left a legacy of service and inspiration.

I read Kennedy's PT 109 book at Clarke Junior High, and then entered a town-wide creative writing contest. To my surprise, I won third place, and my good friend Lexington teacher and Vice Principal, Mr. Larry Robinson, invited me to the Muzzey Junior High to receive an award. My parents were so proud to see my picture in the local newspaper around '77.

Although Mr. Robinson is no longer with us; his memory lives on in the love of his former students, wife and colleagues. He was a special man, and gifted in his interactions with all his students. He loved his students, and they all loved him back. Some teachers are just special human beings that we never forget. I'm certain Mr. Robinson is smiling down from heaven; as I write my books, to help teach a new generation of our youth about America. Mr. Robinson was a treasure to his students, and I always think of the first time I met him whenever I drive by Muzzey Junior High. If you can believe it; I think Mr. Robinson was more proud of me then my parents, the day he handed me that Silver Certificate for creative writing. That's just the man he was. Rest in peace, Mr. Robinson.

President John f. Kennedy before Irish Parliament 1963 (Ireland Public Domain image)

In '63, Kennedy returned our proud US Civil War Irish Brigade colors to the Irish Parliament to great applause and a grand parade down O'Connell Street in Dublin. A beautiful son of Ireland and America, gone too soon, as the world cried with Jackie, and her children.

Dr. Martin Luther King & Senator Robert Kennedy (JFK Presidential Library Public Domain)

The loss of Senator Robert Kennedy and Dr. Martin Luther King was heartbreaking to the nation, but time marches on. Bobby Kennedy once said, "Some see the problems of today and ask why, I see solutions and ask why not?" Dr. Martin Luther King said, "Out of the mountain of despair, a stone of hope." Though Bobby and Martin didn't see their personal dreams realized, a nation greatly mourned their loss but we must feel their eternal blaze on our hearts, and search for that stone of hope. U2 captured this sentiment in their song in the "Name of Love."

Their values and dreams shaped our lives. Service to others is a gift unto itself, and this treasure hunt is a gift to the next generation. In the midst the bad news and negative media of today, we must look back with pride at the good people and their positive examples.

David Valentine Burke received his US Navy Commission at Annapolis from President Kennedy in '61. He was fortunate to play in the USNA Annapolis Band as President John Fitzgerald Kennedy delivered his immortal Inauguration speech. With Barbara Burke by his side, they served their nation and were wonderful parents to their children and grandchildren. They still proudly fly their US Naval Academy, and US flags at their beautiful home overlooking the Atlantic Ocean.

Crypt of Captain John Paul Jones at US Naval Academy (Public Domain)

We, as a family, have toured the US Naval Academy at Annapolis, Maryland. It is a beautiful place; and a great institution for developing future leaders in our Navy, and Marine Corps. John Paul Jones rests in peace there in a beautifully adorned crypt—a great tribute to one of the fathers of the US Navy. I felt honored to be near such a great American hero, and treasure to our nation's history. Was there anyone braver than Captain John Paul Jones?

The Burke's gave me the hand of their gorgeous daughter at a beautiful church, as Saint Brigid smiled upon us. The Cloherty's from Lettercallow, Lettermore County Galway, Ireland, were there and cried tears of joy as the Irish princess bride arrived by horse and carriage to start our marriage. Rain poured and thunder clapped and shook the church. Monsignor John Keilty said the angels were crying tears of joy, and thunder was their applause. He was a special man, great Pastor, and a Lexington Minuteman who wore the prestigious White Tricorne Hat. May God bless his memory, and soul in heaven.

In '61, the 28th Mass Regiment marched with great pride, and so did the 54th Regiment in '65, for the glory of it all. Emerson's essays on self-reliance helped Colonel Robert Gould Shaw of Harvard University fame. His letters still reside there at Harvard. Sadly Shaw's parents' hearts broke upon his gallant charge upon CSA Canon Battery Wagner in Charleston, South Carolina in '65. The 54th Glory Brigade will never be forgotten for their great valor, and sacrifice. Their incredible sculpture rests forevermore on Boston Common under the Massachusetts Governor's Golden Dome. What a treasure.

The sons fought for what their fathers had won, with their last full measure of devotion. Logan said to remember all who fought for liberty's sake on Memorial Day each year. Lincoln stood taller than all men, giving his life to save our nation from its original sin. The angels wept as he spoke at Gettysburg. God bless President Abraham Lincoln who saved our nation from the evil of slavery.

Their iron and glory, the fame now rests with Davis' great heart, powder horn, and his Acton plow. He proudly stood watch to defend that rude bridge for all to see. Day and night he never wavered, nor did Hosmer, beating his drum until he fell, or Blanchard, playing his fife until he was shot as well.

North Bridge Fight (Concord) by Amos Doolittle 1775 (Public Domain)

All died for liberty's sake. Buttrick, who lived right beside there, then screamed out, "Fire? God's sake fire!" It was the shot heard around the world, as the red horde turned and ran.

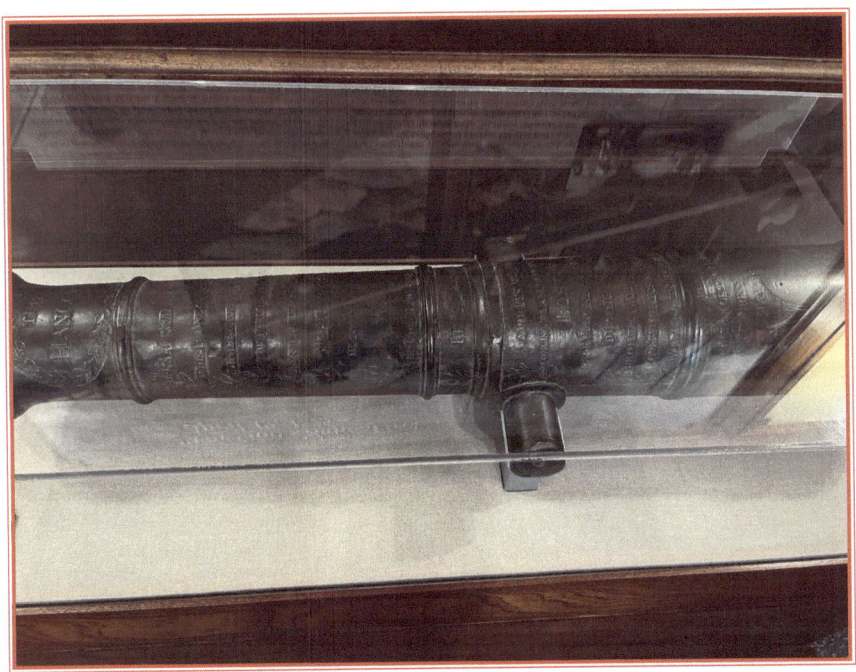

"The Hancock" Cannon – it likely ignited a war (National Park Service Public Domain)

Climb the hill or drive to Liberty Street to see the beautiful gardens, the big map inside, and "The Hancock," which may have started the whole affair, as noted by John Bell's recent book. Gage wanted his stolen brass cannon back, taken from the Boston Common. His spies told Gage they were in Concord.

Next ask the Park Ranger for directions to Barrett's Farm. The Ranger will surely point you on your way. Colonel James Barrett was an extraordinary man. Those brave few faced the greatest foe and awakened the revolutionary spirit that spread all the way to France, who sent their Army and Navy to Rhode Island, New York and Yorktown to aid Washington after the great victory at the Battle of Saratoga. Now the Light of Liberty shines in Paris, and by Ellis Island.

The good ship *Columbia* arrived at Ellis Island with my beloved grandmother, Mary Ann Doherty, escaping oppression from Strabane on the Shannon River in Northern Ireland. When she saw the most beautiful sight she ever saw, she knew everything would be well: *Lady Liberty* greeting her in the harbor, and promising freedom.

Newspaper postings in the 1920 have & earlier made the Irish feel unwelcome (Public Domain)

Without my paternal Grandmother's brave journey, I may not exist. She didn't have much but gave all she had for her children, and Grandchildren. She was truly amazing. Young Mary Ann Doherty knew she would have to work hard to survive. To her sad surprise, she and those she loved still had to overcome "No Irish Need Apply." Irish Catholics were oppressed in Ireland, and sadly in America, too. We had to fight like hell to overcome it. The Irish helped win the American Revolution and US Civil War but still faced discrimination. No one gave the Irish anything; they earned it.

Along this beautiful trail, you feel the chill of yesteryear. But fear not and turn about near the rude bridge. The echo is ringing in your ears as five men fall, Page's flag proudly waving upon the hill. The Redcoats last man was wounded but died by the famous inn. He rests now as folks walk on by.

The wise man retreats so that his far off mother may not cry. The Parson looks down from the Old Manse and shakes his sad head. Off now, head east toward Arrowhead Ridge, Meriam's Meadows, and Carty's Barn for safety, or perhaps not so much after all.

An old Concord Post Card (author's collection)

The Minutemen Militia Companies chose the wetlands path by the fields, wood, and meadows to avoid and flank the King's Troops. All ended up together beyond Author's Ridge, and Arrowhead Ridge. The musket shots then rang out at Meriam's Farm. Both sides would then engage all the way back along that long Battle Road.

Their stones lie about with their red, white, and blue crimson on this well-traveled trail. There are seven or more souls who never got to tell the tale of who fired first. If Woburn's Asahel Porter had survived, he certainly would have the answer to what caused the sympathetic fire by the British Troops, and the dawn of a new nation.

700 – 800 British soldiers facing 1200 – 2000 Provincial Troops (NPS Public Domain)

Head for Brook's place and wet your whistle in his well. It's a long walk back if you're thirsty as hell. Hurry by Hardy's Hill and across Elm Brook near the Bloody Angle. Baldwin arrived with Woburn, and they were hot as hornets after seeing Woburn's son Porter and all of Lexington Minuteman companies dead and wounded. This massacre would not be taken lightly, unlike the Boston Massacre of 1770. Colonel Smith would soon learn it's not wise to mess with the Woburn Tanners.

Battle Road Mural - Minuteman National Historical Park (courtesy of NPS)

With "heavy loads (Forrest Fenn)" and water low, they tried to flee, not so successfully. With more echoes of a musket's blast, some met their end. Poor Mary Hartwell needed an ox and cart to bring them all to their final resting place in the Burying Ground in Lincoln Center.

I dated Sharon Poisson from Wayland back in the 80's. She had a really nice white Monte Carlo SS. We ate Chinese food, then drove around in her cool car with Phil Collins' "In the Air Tonight," Corey Hart's "Sunglasses at Night" & "Never Surrender," Madonna's "Crazy for You," or "Night Moves" by Bob Seger playing on the radio.

Sharon had big brown eyes, a great sense of humor, and a beautiful smile. Being in the West Suburbs, she was young and restless. I did my best to please her every time she took my hand, but I failed her in the end. Our on-and-off relationship was like "The Alcott" sung by The Nationals, and Taylor Swift.

She drove me to the East Sudbury Company's (Wayland) Glezen Rd Training Field, Sudbury Minuteman Statue, Historic First Parish, and we ate dinner at Sudbury's famous Wayside Inn. It's a colonial home where they reenact the Battle of Red Horse Tavern every October, with beautiful lands and an Old Mill surrounding it. I have been there many times throughout my life with those I hold dear. There are many nice colonial events there too. If you visit, you will not be disappointed. Longfellow's Wayside Inn & Sudbury are historical treasures.

We would drive the rural areas of the West Suburbs listening to "Heaven" by Bryan Adams or "Paradise by the Dashboard Lights" by Meatloaf. We ate a lot of Chinese, or Italian food. We also often went for ice cream at Kimball's Farm in Carlisle or Dairy Joy in Weston.

Sharon brought me to historic Boston Post Rd. in Weston Center, and the Old Stone Bridge; not far from her old home on Glezen Lane, Wayland. She pointed out the monument dedicated to General Henry Knox's Troops pulling the cannon on their winter sleds from Fort Ticonderoga New York to General Washington's Headquarters in Cambridge then onto Dorchester Heights. The famous Knox trail is well marked across New York and Massachusetts.

Sometimes she and I would go to Walden Pond in Concord (Henry David Thoreau's Cabin) or Minuteman National Park in Lincoln. Those summer nights are amazing in your late teens or early 20's. Youth is truly wasted on the young.

Sharon proudly told me how the Framingham and Sudbury Minutemen or Militia marched toward Concord, and Lincoln to do battle on that April morn. She said they marched by the Grout-Heard House then put up a great fight near the Bloody Angle in Lincoln. The Sudbury Minutemen still march past their Minuteman Statue on that route each year. Wayland used to be part of East Sudbury, so they took up arms that historic day as well.

Like many young folks; Sharon and I had different dreams, so we took different paths in life but I'm certain she did well. As I walked Sharon out to her car for the last time, she was in tears. She drove away and out of my life in her cool white Monte Carlo SS '85 muscle car. I could hear her radio blasting "It's a Heartache" by Bonnie Tyler. Sharon was not my destiny, and I was not hers. Another would fill those roles for each of us in time.

THE RETREAT FROM LEXINGTON AND CONCORD.

Cornet Page, a local hero of the French Indian War, was waving the company's cavalry flag. Brave Captain Wilson died on the Battle Road in Lincoln as Bedford wept. They raised a monument to Page's memory called "The Patriot" at Veteran's Park.

A proud Bedford Minuteman as Cornet Page Reenactor (photograph by Michael O'Connell)

On April 19, 1775 after the alarm Nathaniel Page left his home at 89 Page Rd., and made his way to Fitch Tavern at 152 Great Rd. Bedford carrying his cavalry flag right past Veterans Memorial Park. The original Bedford Flag is also on display at their town library. What an amazing piece of history Bedford's proud flag. Bedford was among the first to reach Concord, and they gave pursuit back through Lincoln toward Lexington with all their compatriots.

In '23, our old East End crew got together. It was Mike "Asc" Ascolose's turn to buy dinner. So he took Dools, Joe, and me to Bedford House of Roast Beef. It's a small joint, but the food is great, and the folks who work there are nice. I love their steak, extra cheese, and mushroom sub. We ribbed Asc because it was his turn to buy, and he even bought me some Lawton's cookies for the ride home. It's truly special to keep such great lifelong friends and brothers. Too bad Babs couldn't make it, and blew us off once again like a musket's blast.

Asc got burned because he left too fast. Dools and I talked Joe into buying Bedford Farms ice cream. We drove by "The Patriot" with its proud flag flying as it did in Bedford, Concord, Lincoln, Lexington, and perhaps Menotomy, and Cambridge so long ago.

We also passed the famous Bedford Fitch Tavern, where their Minutemen had rallied that April morning. The Bedford Minutemen still proudly carry their flag to all sorts of parades in the area. Lincoln, Bedford and Acton were some of the first units to arrive at Concord so long ago. The June night was perfect under an orange moon as we polished off our ice creams.

18th Royal Irish Regiment Cap Badge (courtesy of Auckland Museum Public Domain)

The relentless foe pursues from behind the Boulder stone. His shot rings out until another foe falls. Those poor souls end up in the ground. The 18th Royal Irish were there, whether they wanted to be or not, on that fateful day. In 1775 all of Ireland was conquered and under the King's rule. An Irish story never has a fairy tale ending.

Now fall back in a hurry at the double-quick, and watch out for Captain Parker hiding among the stones as Colonel Smith leads on by. The Captain lost once before and now will try to even the score, as the Nelson and Whittemore's families duck for cover.

Fiske Farm well pump currently at Munroe Tavern (courtesy of Lexington Historical Society)

Hayward made history by standing his ground near Fiske's Farm well. The place is known for its apple orchard pink blossoms in the spring. Sadly, Hayward ended up under a fine granite stone with a hole shot through his powder horn. Daniel French took note of all these farmers' great bravery. None of their losses were in vain. The Acton Library and Town Hall displays some great relics, but their monument is inaccurate as to where their son, Hayward, actually fell. He was shot at Fiske Farm Old Mass Ave by Wood St. Lexington.

My Aunt Marion Dolan at Tower Park Tattoo (MCV photo)

Remembering the Middlesex County Volunteers and William Diamond's Fife and Drum Corps, fireworks, Coach Bob Farias and Coach Rick Thibeault, shooting summer hoops with Sports Etc squad at Coach Farias' Courts, and loving times with all my family and friends all near Hastings Park, Farias Basketball Courts, Town Pools, and Center Playgrounds abutting LHS.

The legendary Coach Robert "Bob" Farias – I sure miss you (courtesy of the Farias Family)

Perfect moments pass by too quickly, like your beautiful wife walking down the aisle. The town clock never stops its march. As the bridegroom takes his heart's treasure home, you must cherish life and all its pursuits, or the moments will pass by too fast.

Don't get too scared among Ye Olde tombstones; the Tremblay Family will take note and smile as the Grim Reaper passes by. As will the spirits of Amos Doolittle and Mary Ann Doherty because they lived nearby or visited here. My old Lexington friend Ben Nye lived right next door but his parents recently sold their family home. From their homes, they could hear the Belfry Tower ring out every Patriot's Day morning by 5 A.M. as Lexington's children spread the alarm: "The Regulars (British Troops) are out."

Sam Adams and John Hancock left Reverend Clarke's home across Meriam's Hill toward Woburn, and announced, "O. What a glorious morning is this." That enthusiasm for the Patriots earned him a marker on a Meriam Hill stonewall. Sandham's work showed their defiance, even if he embellished it quite a bit. Check it out at nearby Cary Hall on the Old Bay Rd.

At 15, I once got into a tremendous fight in that little park by Fletcher Ave. near the Lexington Police Station. The other guy, Bob Collina, towered over me at perhaps 6'3" or so, and was about twice my weight. Bob used to work at White Hen Pantry in East Lexington and my friends Liza, Stacey and I went in there all the time. I think he was jealous of my beautiful treasured lady friends. He made a really unkind remark I didn't like. I was never short on courage; and had a huge chip on my shoulder, so I recklessly took him on.

I asked him do you want to fight? He said yes. I drew the first punch, and he swung like Thor's hammer but never truly struck home. I twisted, turned, used agility, and soon sent Bob flying to the ground. Those TV wrestling moves from Chief Jay Strongbow, Greg Valentine, and Hulk Hogan really paid off when he hit the ground hard in complete surprise. I felt like Rocky taking on Drago in the "Rocky IV" movie.

Bob was a tough kid. I punched him numerous times in the face, but he kept right on fighting. A lesser opponent would have been finished already. The man could certainly take a punch. He gained my respect as we fought on.

Lt. Bill Dooley likely looked out his commanding officer's window at the Old Police Department building, and sent his officers rolling. Lt. Dooley lived in East Lexington on the Hill. Everyone knew he was a Navy veteran from WWII. He lived first on Bowker St., then Daniels St. My older brother Joe and I used to sled down Bowker Hill on a plastic sled after huge winter storms in the 70's. Joe crashed us directly into a massive iced-up snow bank, which staggered us. We didn't try that again.

Bill Dooley's nephew, Jackie Dooley, has lived his whole life on Baker St. on Liberty Heights. He was a teacher, works at Arlex Oil, and runs Liberty Heights Landscaping. Jackie has a great sense of humor, and we always have a good laugh. I've known his family all my life, so I guess that makes us both "East-Enders" or "Townies." I think we are both equally proud of that. Jackie is a great guy.

They knocked down the old police building, and now there's a new Police Station. Bob and I ended up calling the fight a draw when the cops came calling, but since I was much smaller, that was kind of a win. My friend David Radlo from LHS Football was there. He said, "Okie, you certainly have courage."

Bobby Collina went on to become a career US Marine Corps Sergeant; so he is definitely tougher than me, and I salute his service to our nation. We used to run into each other at the Avenue Barber Shop in the

East End often. His brother Ed was the Melrose Fire Chief. I was always proud to have grown up near them in the East Lexington. They certainly did their share of hanging out and sledding at the "Piggy" or playing at Sutherland Park. They likely drank some beer there too but they never caused anyone issues so all is good. The Collina boys were more great examples of Adams School pride.

LHS 1981 Graduate US Army Colonel Robert McClaughlin, Ret. (courtesy of McClauglin Family)

Retired Concord Police Chief Barry Neal and I marched with my scout son, Corey, in the Lexington Veterans Day parade from the historic Munroe Cemetery to the Town Common. We marched with honor with our LHS Class of '81 brother, US Army Colonel Robert "McCluke" McClaughlin, Ret. Bob was honored as the Grand Marshall of the parade. Talk about tough as nails serving throughout active war actions overseas. A great Adams School product that served over 20 years answering his nation's call in foreign wars. Robert also played football and earned his varsity letter. He was another winner from the very beginning.

Bob's mom was nice to us as little kids. I remember her yummy "piggies in a blanket" at lunchtime on Thursdays. May she rest in peace with her friend, my mother Brigid. Those East Lexington mothers were special. Their husbands were tough blue-collar workers but it never seemed to bother our mothers too much.

My friend Andy MacAleer, a gifted writer and US Army Sergeant, put together a volume of recipes and named the book in honor of our East Lexington Mothers. Andy was right; our East Lexington mothers were the best!

Andy lives on Follen Hill with his older brother Jay, who served in the US Marine Corps. Their parents were wise Irish Catholics and left their home to their son for legacy's sake. That's a hell of a lot smarter than selling your beloved home to some stranger. The money will fade away over time but ties to a community can go on and on. Interestingly, Aiden Lassell Ripley lived at 52 Follen Rd for over 30 years painting in his studio there!

We all loved our East End Barber at Avenue Barber Shop. Victor Iocco was everyone's friend. He cut all our hair for 30 or 40 years or more. His place was right next to Bellino's All-American Donut Shop.

Lady Liberty's Treasure Hunt

by Michael Cloherty O'Connell

Somewhere on this map,
"Lady Liberty's Treasure" is waiting
for you under starry skies.
Please safely enjoy "Lady Liberty's Chase"
and adventure with your family & friends...

Cornwall

Brockville

Saint Lawrence

Kingston

Watertown

ADIRONDAC PARK

Mt

Lake G
Gle

LAKE ONTARIO

Rochester

Utica

Northum
Sarat
Spri

Niagara
Falls

Finger Lakes

Syracuse

Mohawk

Schenectady

Buffalo ○ Bennington ★

NEW YORK

Albar

Kinde

LAKE ERIE

Ithaca

CATSKILL
PARK
Slide Mtn ★

Kingston
Catskill Mtn
Railroad

Erie
90

Jamestown

Elmira

Binghamton

Poughkeepsie

ALLEGHENY
NAT'L
FOREST

Williamsport

Scranton

Vails
Gate

87

80

Wilkes
Barre

Susquehanna

Delaware

Battle
Sleepy Hollow

Dobbs
Ferry

Beaver
Falls

PENNSYLVANIA

76

Freedom

Allegheny

State
College

Altoona
99

Johnstown

476

81

Phillipsburg

Ford
Mansion
Morristown

Delaware River Railroad ★

Statue of Liberty
& Ellis Island

Ne

Pittsburgh

76

Monongahela

70

79

Harrisburg ✦
Carlisle

Lancaster

Allentown

78

Liberty Hall

Valley
Forge

83

York

Railroad Museum
of Pennsylvania ★

Princeton
Battle
Monument ★

Washington's
Delaware
Crossing ★

Trenton Battle Monum

Trenton

Sachs Covered Bridge
Eisenhower Farm ○ Gettysburg
Fairfield

Battlefield, Museum, &
National Military Park

Chadds
Ford

Philadelphia ○

Carpenter's Hall
& Liberty Bell Center

95

9

WEST

Morgantown

Cumberland

Wilmington

NEW

Hagerstown

MARYLAND

JERSEY

Public-Access Lands, Historic Places & Parks

DEL

13

Dover

Atlantic
City

0   25   50   100   177.6   200 miles

Cape
May

MAINE

Presque Isle

Houlton

BAXTER STATE PARK

Mt Katahdin

Calais

Bangor
Brewer

Downeast Scenic Railroad

Andover

Lovejoy Covered Bridge

Waterville

Ellsworth

Bar Harbor

Comstock Covered Bridge

Fairfax Covered Bridge

Vermont Scenic Trains

Essex Junction

WHITE MTNS NF

Augusta

Lewiston

Vermont State House

Mt Washington

Jackson
Jackson Falls

Bartlett

Conway Scenic Railroad

VERMONT

Joshua Chamberlain Monument at Bowdoin College

Portland

Lebanon

Cornish-Windsor Covered Bridge

NEW HAMPSHIRE

Concord

Piscataqua River Bridge

Kittery

Badger's Island

Rye Beach

Stark Farm

Manchester

Robert Frost Farm

Phillips Academy

Chelmsford

Rockport

Gloucester

Acton Centre

Minuteman Statue

Salem

Lechmere Square

Acton Davis Farm

The Battle Road Trail & Minute Man NHP

Old North Church

In Beacon Hill, Boston
Boston State House
Boston Common
Robert Gould Shaw
& the 54th Regiment Memorial

Worcester

Boston

MASS

Springfield

Old Connecticut Path

Plymouth Rock

Cape Cod

Providence

Hartford

RI

New Bedford

East Hampton

Portsmouth

Grand Bellevue Rail

Battle of Quaker Hill

Newport

White Horse Tavern

Essex Steam Train & Riverboat

New Haven

Westerly

Aquidneck Island

CONN

London

Watch Hill

Martha's Vineyard

Nantucket Island

Bridgeport

Island

ATLANTIC OCEAN

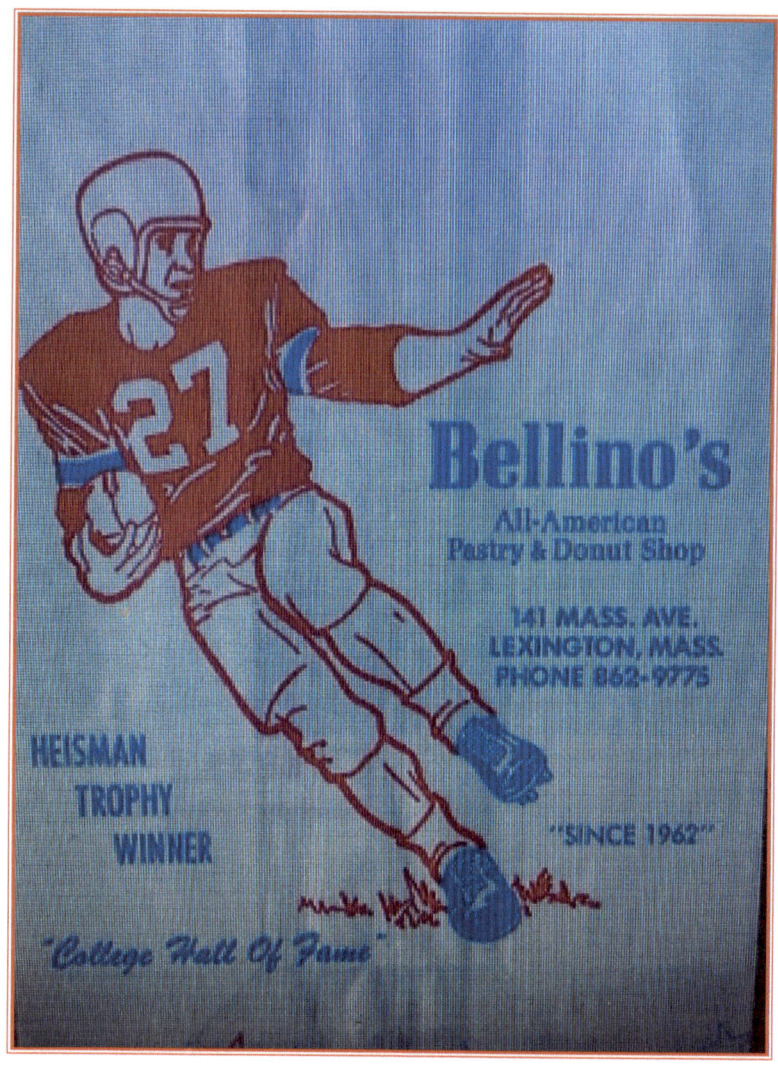

One of the old Bellino's donut bags (courtesy of the Bellino Family)

Steve Barentine lived on Taft Ave by Daniels St in the Family home near Lt. Bill Dooley's home. He worked at Bellino's (current renovated Dunkin Donuts) at night making the donuts. I was friendly with him and Victor. Steve would hang around the Avenue Barber Shop and chat sports. Mr. B., as everyone in East Lexington called him, ran the Adams Summer Playground, too. He loved baseball and coached the best team in town, the Mets. He had an eye for recruiting talented players and loved to win. Victor sponsored his team every year, so the Avenue Barber Shop had a bunch of Mets Baseball Championship trophies from years back.

Me and Coach Rudy Hoiseth at former Adams School baseball field (photo by Joe O'Connell)

I played a lot of baseball growing up in Lexington, and I had to improve so much over the years. One of my favorite baseball coaches was Mr. Rudy Hoiseth of the Bulls when I was very young. He loved me for some reason and made me an all-star player in the game played among all the teams at Adam's School baseball field. It meant so much to me, and gave me confidence. I think from that point on, I was always an all-star baseball player on the teams I played on. Youth coaches matter so much to the young people playing on their teams. I will never forget Coach Rudy. May he rest in peace. I am still close friends with Rudy's son Bryan, and his lovely wife Michelle. Bryan Hoiseth sent me the scan of this photograph my Dad gave his father in the early 70's. The Hoiseth's own a nice house, barn and horse farm in Bedford not far from the area rail trails.

One morning when I was 13, I walked in to see Victor and Mr. B. as they drank their morning coffee. Mr. B. decided it was time to "raz" me because my middle-of-the-road Angels were playing his first place Mets that evening at my school, Clarke Junior High. He and Victor had quite the laughs at my expense as Mr. B. explained how bad my team was and that they were going to kill us that evening. I responded back politely, and respectfully to my elders that it would be a good game.

I think Mr. B's words came back to haunt him that night. I was batting cleanup, and in the 9th inning, we were losing by a run with 2 outs. We had a man on base at 1st and 2nd, and their star pitcher was losing his confidence. It was my turn to bat. I slowly walked up to the plate looking at Mr. B. the whole time; as he sat on the 1st base side, and stared back at me. I waited for my pitch, and it came—a fastball. I crushed it out of play into the bushes in left field. It should have been a home run but the umpire told me to run it out.

I chose to slowly walk up the baseline instead and just look at Mr. B. as our two base runners crossed all their bases to score 2 more runs. Then I stepped on 1st base, and the umpire signaled the game was over. The Angels had beaten the 1st place Mets.

The next morning, I walked into the Avenue Barber Shop and saw Mr. B. and Victor. Mr. B. did not eat humble pie very well. He proceeded to say how bad my team was but that I was one of the best players in the league. I disagreed about my friends on the Angels, but Mr. B. and I remained friends. Steve and Victor have been gone for a while now. I miss them and have never been able to return to the Avenue Barber Shop because Victor and his close friend Freddy are no longer there. They cut my hair from the time I was about 4 years old until I was at least 44 or older. I wept when Victor passed. He was always a positive part of my life. May Victor, and Mr. B. rest in peace. I hope they are watching a good baseball game together in heaven.

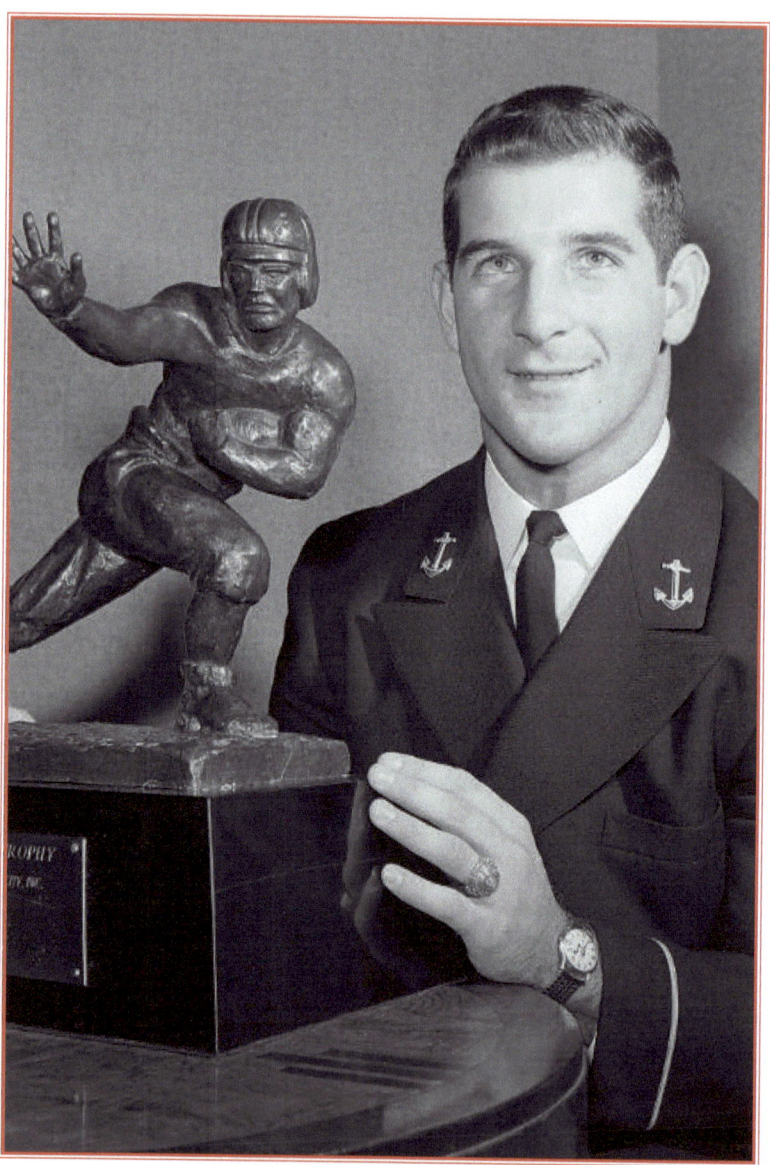

US Naval Academy Graduate Joe Bellino Winchester, MA (USNA Public Domain)

Bellino's All American Donut Shop was named in honor of their cousin, USNA graduate Joe Bellino from Winchester, who won the Heisman Trophy and then served in the Navy. Veto Bellino's son Mark is a Lexington Firefighter. Mark was a good athlete in his day, especially at 1st base. Peter "Rock" Scopa is Mark's uncle.

Another of my friends in the Lexington Fire Department is Paul Bates. He was a three-sport varsity athlete and Captain of the Class of 1980 football, hockey, and baseball teams. You could not have a better friend. Paul grew up off Wood St. near Minuteman National Park. Every time Paul sees me he yells "Okie" out the window of his car. That always makes me smile.

Wood St. is named for Lexington Minuteman Sylvanus Wood, who captured a towering British Grenadier on April 19, 1775, and had another person march him back to Lexington Common at the point of his musket barrel. Sylvanus Wood was really brave, being half the other man's size. I have spent a lot of time in Minuteman National Park. I would park my car by Old Mass Ave and Wood St., then either hike the area or use my mountain bike to exercise. It's a beautiful park and a solid 5 1/2 or 6 miles to Meriam's Corner in Concord, MA. Many people exercise and enjoy this historic trail.

So when you arrive in Lexington Center, Rancatore's Ice Cream is on the corner. My lifelong friend Mark McCullough lives nearby. He loves Lexington so much he became President of the Lions Club. We used to play baseball with his brother Bobby "Pudge" McCullough. Pudge was their catcher; I was on the opposing team. Doug Lucente lives near Mark. He loves Lexington too, as a Lexington Lion - Past President and Selectman. Good for both of my friends, I salute their lifetime community service to Lexington.

Passing "O'Connell's Corner" next, officially named by the Town of Lexington Select Board long ago at the corner of Mass Avenue and Winthrop Road but long forgotten by the current Board of Selectmen, not even a sign to remember my great, great Uncle Daniel O'Connell who served Lexington on the Celebration's Committee for a great many years. Dr. Prescott had passed by here so long ago too on that night he was out late courting Miss Lydia Mulliken.

A View of the South Part of Lexington by Amos Doolittle 1775 (Public Domain)

The smell of Lydia Mulliken's dwelling, shop, and another burnt home still fills the air, as Historical Artist Amos Doolittle identified so long ago.

Reenactment of Percy's cannon covering retreat along the Old Bay Road (photo by author)

Lydia's Mulliken's brother was wounded on the Lexington Common, and later died from his wound. Lydia's beloved Dr. Samuel Prescott was a High Son of Liberty. He had reported to Sam Adams and John Hancock at Hancock Clarke House on April 18, 1775 of Concord's disposition, and that the brass cannon and supplies were safely away to Acton, Groton, or Stow. Later that night, Dr. Prescott acted as a warning rider.

Storming Fort Ticonderoga 1775 by Frederic Remington (NY Library Public Domain)

Dr. Prescott would treat all the wounded on April 19, 1775 including his brother Abel, then join the Continental Army as a medic. He went with General Henry Knox to Fort Ticonderoga, and Prescott helped liberate Boston from the British siege with Knox's captured guns.

General Henry Knox trail is marked from New York to Massachusetts (Public Domain)

They dragged those cannons all the way back from Fort Ticonderoga along the Henry Knox Trail marked from the Lake George and Saratoga area through Old Post Road in Weston, Massachusetts. Those guns were delivered to General George Washington at his headquarters in Cambridge, Massachusetts, right in Harvard Square then onto Dorchester Heights. These are important places to visit, and study American history.

Lydia Mulliken waited for her love, Dr. Samuel Prescott, to return to her, but sadly she never married her beloved. Prescott had volunteered as a Continental Navy privateer. The British in the North Atlantic captured his ship, and he was sent to prison in Halifax, Nova Scotia. Prescott died there from cold, and starvation in 1777. The Prescott and Mulliken families paid a very high price for our freedom and liberty.

Paul O'Connell & Michael Ascolese at Patriot's Day parade by Old Russell House (author photo)

I remember sitting on the rock wall at the Russell House Mass Ave near Woburn St. with my loving Grandma Mary Ann (Doherty) O'Connell at my side, listening to the fife and drums, as the patriotic flags unfurled proudly in April's parade. The Spirit of '76 always leads the way.

Major General Warren arrived just before another wiser foe named Lord Hugh Percy. But there was no escaping the shadow of the gun. The Meeting House and Harrington House were hit by enemy fire, producing terror as the brave took flight, and the enemy withdrew on the path of A. Lassell Ripley's great works.

Warren tried desperately to rally his men to press their pursuit. "Keep a brave heart. They began it; but see to it, lads, that we end it."

Stop into the Lexington Post Office as you pass by to mail the postcards you collected along the way. Ask the postal workers about Ripley's art mural. I'm certain they know him well. If they can't help you, perhaps ask the reference desk at the Cary Memorial Library about A. Lassell Ripley and Amos Doolittle's art works.

A young couple going to the Lexington Center 1794 Mass Ave Movie Theatre (Public Domain)

I went to a great movie with Mary Pawlak in Lexington Center in '83 called "Raiders of the Lost Ark." Ironically, my wife Laurel worked there; I think she sold us the movie tickets that evening. Harrison Ford in the movie said, "All treasure hunting begins in the library with research." That's really good advice for treasure searchers.

If I were you, I would watch "Indiana Jones and the Last Crusade" and both "National Treasure" movies to help you get into the spirit before you attempt Lady Liberty's Treasure Hunt.

Mary loved to swim and did drama. I proudly took her to her prom in my red Dodge sedan. Cindy Lauper sang "True Colors," and we were all "Footloose." Everyone there was young and beautiful. I saw my future beautiful wife Laurel at this prom, too with all her friends. "Making Love Out of Nothing At All" by Air Supply pretty much explained these late teenage years. I was still "Waiting for a Star to Fall" (Boy Meets Girl), and so was Laurel.

Mary was really smart; and went off to Boston College, where my future wife Laurel was studying. We were all close friends for about ten years. Our hearts broke when cancer took Mary far too young at 27 from all who loved her. I still regularly visit her Westview Cemetery grave. I remained close to her wonderful parents, Marilyn and Bob (sadly passed away in July 2023). Mary's sister Julie is a dear friend, too. She still lives in our hometown with her husband and daughters.

Mary is buried close to another dear friend of mine that I regularly visit as well, Carolyn McCabe, who died in 1986 at only 21 in a tragic car accident. Carolyn was a three-sport super athlete. She and I would often shoot hoops together outside at Adams School or at the Center Courts. Carolyn had a sweet, an easy way about her. I loved her smile and laughter. Even on the hottest summer days, she could talk me into playing hoops. God, did everyone love her. Carolyn regularly beat me at one on one basketball, and became Co Captain of Lexington's Girl's Division 1 Varsity basketball team.

Losing my dear friend Carolyn in the summer of '86 was a crushing blow. Life is so precious and fragile. When I think back to losing Carolyn and then Mary, I can still feel the loss and pain expressed in Bonnie Tyler's famous song "Total Eclipse of the Heart." I miss my friends but hope and pray that when it's my time,

I may see them both again in God's house. In my mind's eye, I can hear the Goo Goo Dolls song "Name" quietly playing "It's lonely where you are. Come back down, and I won't tell them your name."

Back to 1775 Colonel Smith and Major Pitcairn came here uninvited. They must have treasured General Percy's arrival in Lexington on his white horse with his relief column and field pieces. Percy tried to help Smith; and Pitcairn's troops fall back by burning several homes, and providing cover fire but they all soon fled east for safety toward Munroe's place. Sgt. Munroe must have been quite displeased when they took over his home.

With anger and rage in their hearts, poor Raymond never had a chance. In fear, unarmed Raymond tried to escape by the rear door. He was then shot and killed. Major Pitcairn did not fare much better; by June 17, he was sleeping forever in Boston's Christ Church tomb, popularly known as the Old North Church.

Washington and Lafayette both rode on past here on their own to a hero's welcome sometime much later. So did Grant and Ford in '75. The Belfry clangs for freedom's voice. Like a Blue Knight on a Holy Grail Quest, never stop searching until you find that which you seek.

The pursuit is on to capture Burke's heart back to '83. I placed some 1965 silver coins in the treasure chests in honor of her birth year. I put in 1963 coins for my own birth year, too. Good luck finding them. I am not parting with it too easily. So don't be too slow or go off unprepared.

For all pretty teenage girls, time keeps passing by with the clank of the stairs. They smile, wink, and flirt just a bit. Their young man waits patiently for his love's smile and to take her hand. We all remember those days fondly. Young teenage years laughing, smiling, movies, dances, and just hanging out as you try to grow up and learn about life. "Lucky" dated "Ang." "Ando" dated Jamie. "Kiki" dated Jill. Ben dated Chris. For me, it was an exceptionally cute blonde with a great smile - Liza Baumgartner. I got lost in Liza's big brown eyes; and all her charms on the Old Boston and Maine railroad bridge over Grant St., close to where she grew up.

Liza and her best friend Stacey Shepard were a big part of my life in '79. Wherever they wanted to go, Lucky and I would happily follow. Sometimes we would walk east on Mass Ave by Pelham Rd to the park in the summer. The very beautiful girls would sunbathe in the park, in their bikinis lying on towels. The passing guys must have been jealous of the treasures we had found because they were always beeping their horns at Liza and Stacey or whistling. The young ladies did not seem to mind the attention, and pretty much learned to ignore it.

It was true love forever. When Liza kissed me for the first time on Grant Street, I felt lightning strike my heart, so that became her nickname for me alone. I was her Romeo, and she was my Juliet, like the Taylor Swift "Love Story" song. I loved Liza deeply, and she loved me back with all her heart. I thought our love would be timeless. Maybe every young man thinks that about their first girlfriend?

Teenage love in '78 and '79 was perfume, makeup, Bubblicious chewing gum, Star Wars & Grease movies, ET, Reese's Pieces, Root Beer floats, "Angie," "Sympathy for the Devil," and "Gimme Shelter" by the Rolling Stones, Led Zeppelin, Aerosmith, Boston, The Knack, Supertramp, The Cars, Styx, Fleetwood Mac, Don Henley, The Eagles, Cheap Trick, Pink Floyd, and Rush always playing in the background. When you're young, the summers seem to last forever; but then again, they pass by too fast like a shooting star.

Love is passionate and not for the meek of heart. Liza and I dated while Cheap Trick at Budokan played on the radio, "I Want You to Want Me." I loved her so much, and never wanted to lose her.

She was my first real girlfriend, and I had much to learn about women. Liza and I fought over stupid stuff, but we were really just another "Brick in the Wall" (Pink Floyd), trying to earn our high school diplomas, and fit in like everyone else. We had to find our place on this Earth.

We both had to try to overcome significant challenges at home. Liza had tragically lost her mom far too young in a car accident. She had a picture of her mom on the wall, and she was beautiful, like Meryl Streep. Liza had her mother's good looks and charm. My mother Brigid was chronically ill, so that was really hard on me. This all made me feel like the amazing Switchfoot song: "Dare you to Move."

High school teaches you lessons; like life is hard, and not always fair. I learned many lessons about this by playing sports. My Lexington High JV football team travelled to Lincoln Sudbury High School for an exhibition game. Final score: Home 0 Visitors 24. I embarrassed myself getting too mad at my zero playing time, and would have preferred to be with beautiful girlfriend Liza.

We then faced Concord Carlisle High School at Concord in another exhibition game. They had zero chance of beating us. Lexington was in a higher sport's division then Concord Carlisle. The final score was Concord 17 and Lexington 42. I wondered why the Athletic Directors would schedule such an uneven athletic contest.

Then we faced Minuteman Vocational High School on the Lexington and Lincoln line. Their athletic fields were in Lincoln back then. We were a much bigger school, so the match was unfair. The whole game ended up being another big zero for me. Final score: Home 17 Visitors 31. We won but it seemed very unfair to me. I felt bad for the other team.

The next game we traveled to Lincoln Sudbury High School for a real game, and they won 10 to 7 because sadly Bob McLaughlin #76 on our team got injured, and it through off the whole game for our offense. The coaches were not happy so after we shook hands; we ran drills after the game, and then got a lecture before getting on the bus.

The bus got back late to LHS. I showered quickly, and missed showing up on time for a date with Liza. God, I loved her, and I would rather have missed that Football game in Sudbury but that was not an option. Miss a game or practice without approval, and you're off the team.

I tried to explain to my girl what happened, and she cut me off. Her father wouldn't let her go out late so Liza told me "I was nothing but a dumb jock." She wasn't wrong. It was a stark reality to have to address my inherent weaknesses. "In a New York Minute" (Don Henley), she would soon be gone from my life. Losing Liza was a crushing blow; she truly was the most important person, and a treasure to me at that time in my life.

I guess we all have a history or a past that is important to us, even if it's not significant to others. As the Seasons pass and die, then a new season begins. Liza's love for me died, and I truly did not understand why. Were young women or was love itself just fickle?

She never cared to explain, and I never dared to ask. I felt like the Lewis Capaldi song, "I was getting kind of used to being someone you loved." Then it came to an end. I felt crushed like in the Passenger song and had to "Let Her Go."

My only interests around '79 were football, soccer, basketball, baseball, Liza, and professional sports. That year, my Reds baseball team won the championship at Center 4. I proudly wore the coat our Coach Walter Johnson gave us that season.

The Cars were on the radio with their "Moving in Stereo" and "All Mixed Up" compilation songs. Aerosmith and Boston bands were getting some good competition. J. Geils was also rocking it, singing "Love Stinks." At that point in my life, I agreed.

The next young lady that took my interest was Emily Tutun. She was a cute, athletic, and curvy brunette. What a cutie. She would flirt with me and drive me absolutely crazy. She knew it, too. Oh, the power of a beautiful woman. I went to many of her softball and field hockey games to cheer for her. She did not mind that I loved sports, and her brother was on my Championship baseball team.

Reds 1979 Champions at Lexington Center 4 Ball Field (photograph by Joseph F. O'Connell)

Emily came to some of our Reds baseball games. She always came over to see me after the games were over but her parents kept her close at hand. I was pretty certain that they did not want her to date me. This may have explained her reluctance.

Emily came from a wealthy, Jewish family. She was busy attending Hebrew School while I was getting confirmed as a Roman Catholic. I came from a poor Irish family, quite literally on the other side of the tracks from her because she grew up on Tyler Rd. I gave Emily the Billy Joel Breaking Glass album and told her the song "You May Be Right" was about us.

She smiled, and happily went about her life. She was ready to conquer the world but made no time for me. I know she got married and moved to Newton. I hope she found a great guy that does not drive her too crazy. "All of My Love" by Led Zeppelin was a really popular radio song at that time.

I was young, fit, and would run with fire burning bright beneath my feet; the 5-mile route, sometimes every day of the week. Down Sylvia St., Mass Ave to Bow St., Rawson Rd. to Lillian Rd., onto Lowell St. by the Shaw's family home at 219 Lowell Street (Jim, Robert, and Chuck were all my friends). Jim recently earned the White Tricorne Hat Award. His dad, Dick, would have loved that because he was President of the Lexington Lions Club. My brothers Paul, and John were good friends with Billy and Jeff Shaw and their sisters, too.

I would then run by Winchester Dr., near Emily Tutun's Tyler Rd. home, then pass my friends Jimmy and Chris Casey's childhood home, then northwest toward Woburn St. I was like Matthew Modene in the famous *Visionquest* movie with "Lunatic Fringe" by Red Ryder, "Change" by John Waite, and Journey's "Only the Young" playing in my headphones as I ran.

I would pass by Webb St. My father grew up at 74 Webb St. with his brother Charles, sisters Marion and Peggy. The last house on the left. They played in the Lower Vinebrook Conservation Land as children. I spent time there too, chasing butterflies or helping my Uncle Paul and Aunt Marion Dolan with their garden behind Eleanor Modono's Woburn St home. The Modono family had a farm there for many years; now it's a Church of Latter-Day Saints. I'm still friends with DJ and Anthony Modono. They are a great Lexington family.

I would then run by friend Krissy French's home on Woburn St. Her grandmother, Bette Rycroft, was a really nice lady. I would look down Utica St. toward Neil Cronin's house. He was just amazing and loved Lexington's history so much.

Lifetime Lexington resident Bobby Frissore – we miss you Bobby (Courtesy of John Frissore)

One of my great aunts, Margaret O'Connell, lived steps away on Dunham Rd. When I was a teenager, we had campfires hanging out by the pond on the Lower Vinebrook Conservation Land or at adjacent Ash's Hill. My father hung out here as well when he was a teenager, too. He was friendly with Bob Frissore, who lived close by over on Young St. Bobby had a 1954 Green Belair that he proudly drove around town. He was a very happy man and was always smiling or laughing.

The Frissore's are a great Lexington family. One of their clan, John, lives in East Lexington on the Old Bay Road. John told me that he loved that the alarm riders went right by his residence on April 18, 1775. The Red Coats passed by there, too.

My Grandfather WW1 Private Charles James O'Connell (Family photograph)

After my Grandfather, WWI era US Army Private Charles James O'Connell, died too young in '43, my Grandma moved to 47 Woburn St. to be closer to the schools, Saint Brigid's Church, and the Center of Town. This put Muzzey & Munroe Schools short walks away from the house for all her children on the other side of the active railroad tracks.

Their house would shake when the trains went by. My widowed Grandma O'Connell lived there until 1990 when she passed to God's kingdom. I think her husband must have been waiting patiently for her in heaven because she never dated another man after losing him. That's love but also very sad, too.

I'd always stop for a pit stop and say hi to my Grandma, Uncle Paul, and Aunt Marion (O'Connell) Dolan. They were all very important to me. I would drink water or OJ then carry on. Off to Mass Ave; diagonally across the street from the home my grandfather Charles James O'Connell grew up at 1536 Mass Ave., an old beautifully preserved Colonial. I met the owners at 1536 Mass Ave and complimented on how well the maintained their home. I love all their patriotic banners on Patriot's Day, and July 4th. My Grandfather's Uncle lived directly behind them on 1 Winthrop Rd. Two O'Connell brothers side by side.

Then I would run east at full speed down Munroe Hill, past the park, then Follen Church in the East Village, my friend Bobby Blood's family home on Mass Ave., and back to Berman's Liquor Store parking lot to stretch out. Not much has changed back there in the last 45 years or so; except for the sad fact that many of our parents are gone, and their homes are getting knocked down for the sake of progress. My parent's home is gone now; their property at 15 & 17 Sylvia St was made into a nice duplex. The home that Mike Ascolese grew up in at 18 Sylvia St. is still there. I really like that the old Coyne and Babineau family homes are still there just completely modernized with additions.

My older brother Joe was at Bentley University Waltham, and I at Northeastern University Boston. We were both commuter students because we could not afford to live at college, and had to work to pay our way in life. Our parents could not help us at all. My parents could barely help themselves. I left my parents' home with the shirt on my back and a toothbrush. Joe and I got an apartment at 1475 Mass. Ave. We both had to get out there, and work hard.

Kind of sad, our youngest brother John was the last O'Connell to live in Lexington. The Town just got too affluent for all of us, I guess. The O'Connell's had lived there back to 1840. John lives in God's home now with our parents, and ancestors.

"It seemed to me (John) lived his life like a candle in the wind. Never knowing who to turn to when the rain set in" (Elton John). It was truly sad; John died as I held his hand, prayed for his soul, and cried.

In my mind's eye, I could hear "Purple Rain" by Prince playing "I only wanted to see you laughing in the Purple Rain." John had diabetes and drank far too much. That was the end of John, with his beautiful kind heart. I sure do miss your laughter, John. Rest in peace forevermore, my beloved baby brother.

The tears sometimes never stop. Some people from our lives can never be replaced. Likely, John is making everyone at God's table laugh at this moment. Maybe he is looking down now, smiling as I remember him.

Lightning broke my heart in '79 but that is often how young love goes. You can't fully express or show young women how you feel at 15 or 16 but you can love them in your heart just the same. "With no loving in our songs; and no money in our coats, you can't say we are satisfied" (Rolling Stones).

Liza moved on to several different stiffs. They were all kind of losers but that was her call to make. I'm sure she was well aware I did not respect any of her choices in new boyfriends. They certainly were not athletes. I wanted to beat the guff out of those guys rather badly because they were all bad influences on someone I loved at the time. But Liza was very strong-willed; and would have gotten really mad at me, so I sadly just walked on in life. My favorite Rolling Stones song "Angie" still reminds me of that special place in time.

"But Angie, I still love you baby. Everywhere I look I see your eyes. There ain't a woman that comes close to you. Come on baby, dry your eyes. Angie, ain't it good to be alive. Angie, Angie, you can't say we never tried" (Rolling Stones).

I wonder if Liza still remembers me when she hears "Angie" on the radio? It's hard to know; perhaps she meant more to me than I did to her back in '79. Fair enough; she was smarter, kinder, and more beautiful with her beautiful blond hair, and those big brown eyes. I ran into her father Dick a few years later in the early 80's. He kind of hated me with good reason; when I dated his daughter, because she loved me too much.

He mentioned he could not stand any of her new boyfriends since me, and wished I'd take Liza out again. I was surprised then told him simply that Liza had lost interest in me long ago, and stopped being my friend. I further said, "So I guess, I was not so bad after all." He agreed, and we laughed. He is now in heaven with his wife again. I hope they are both happy in God's home looking down on their children and grandchildren.

Time has an odd way of changing folks' points of view. So those loser guys somehow raised my stock or perhaps he would not like any guy while Liza was a young woman? Fair enough, I'd say. He was just a father protecting his daughter.

Liza married a really nice guy from Lexington. They moved to Groton, and had a couple of kids. Liza deserved all the happiness in the world, and she eventually found it. They even have a nice family home on Cape Cod. Good for Liza, no one on this Earth deserves happiness more than her.

I then dated Liza's friend Stacey Shepard. She loved to skate at Hayden Ice Rink but how could she ever frustrate me. Stacey was a beautiful young lady with an athlete's figure. Boy, did she love to tease. "She's Always a Woman" by Billy Joel was a popular song back then.

A really Old Postcard; one-cent postage, of Belfry Hill (Author's postcard collection)

Never under estimate the power of a woman. Stacey talked me into sledding down Belfry Hill toward the Old Hancock School even though I tried to tell her it was unsafe. Stacey said, "No Mike, we are doing it" so I had to agree. The cliff had insufficient snow so we soon crashed, and got thrown quite badly. The blood poured from my face as Stacey laughed. She said to put some snow and ice on that. Stacey had a great sense of humor, that's for certain. Stacey was the Queen of Diamonds. She always made me feel like the Bryan Adams song: "When you love someone."

Stacey was a true beauty and had really great curves that turned all the guys' heads. I unwisely called her "Trans Am" referring to her curves. She didn't like that very much and used her clog shoe in such a way to express herself, and I buckled in pain.

She broke up with me within six months or so. She said I was "Little Boy Blue, that never does anything wrong." She further said that I always loved Liza more than her. Ouch, I knew I was in deep trouble with that comment. I did not say it but thought to myself; that Liza loved me more than Stacey did as well, so turnabout was fair play.

Further, I had made the huge mistake of always giving Liza gold jewelry, then Stacey silver jewelry just to mix things up a bit. Stacey did not deserve to feel like I put her in second place, and I knew in my heart she was right. I brought Stacey lots of flowers but that did not change her mind a bit. I was past history to Stacey who said we could be friends but that never really goes well.

Losing Stacey hurt. I felt like the Callum Scott song "Dancing on My Own." Stacey found a new boyfriend easily because she was very beautiful, friendly and a true charmer. We remained friends but I could never figure out why I always got her upset with me. Likely she will read this, and not like it very much as well. See I have proven my point; I just managed to upset her again. Just kidding. Stacey deserves the best, and I truly hope she finds it.

I forgave Stacey and Liza long ago, and in my 1981 yearbook, I said goodbye to "Lightning," "Trans Am," and Coach Bob Farias. I truly loved them all. That was over 45 years ago now but yet it seems like yesterday. Stacey also moved out to the Groton area, and had a couple of really nice children. Her daughter; who is a beauty just like her mom, just got married. Wow, time flies. I wish we could all go back to 1975 and do it all again.

Don Henley had it right in the Eagle's song "Desperado." "Don't you draw the Queen of Diamonds; Boy, she'll beat if she's able. The Queen of Hearts is always your best bet." So I kept right on dating in the years ahead, searching for the Queen of Hearts.

I was actually truly sad on my graduation day in '81 to leave so many dear friends behind. Also, I felt I had not done a damn thing in life yet, and my father was forcing me to attend the very worst college around as a commuter student, and pay for it myself of course. It really was not pleasant being poor.

Oddly enough, I became best friends with Stacey's Dad "Shep" on Fletcher Ave. Like most fathers, he didn't like me much when I was dating Stacey. But that all changed after we broke up, and married others.

That devil; Shep with his angelic wife, Dee (Shepard Family photograph)

Shep and I have laughed together for hours on end. He is kind of a devil and often says, "thank God, you didn't marry my daughter," with a sort of evil grin. His religious; and angelic wife Dee looks into the den, and just shakes her head. We both become very quiet and careful, trying not to commit any further sins.

I also dated a hazel-green-eyed beauty; lets call her "Ms. Misery" like the great song by Elliot Smith at the end of movie *God Will Hunting*. She was very important to me, and was a favorite of my mother because she came from Irish Catholic parents. She was very religious, and her parents were really strict. Miss Misery had a great personality, and she always made me smile.

Our relationship was like Norman and Jessie in the famous Brad Pitt movie: *The River Runs Through It*. This great girl even looked like Jessie, with the same great smile, happy eyes, and charm. Her parents made certain that me, and any other guy that came along stayed far away from their High School age daughter. They chaperoned the whole night any time I visited their home.

This adorable young lady loved Bruce Springsteen and Bread. "Aubrey," "Because the Night," and "Thunder Road" were her favorite songs. I preferred "Jungleland" by the Boss - Bruce Springsteen. I owned the Bruce Springsteen and the E Street Band Greatest Hits CDs. The Boss rocks! I was not a big Bread fan. I specially framed "Aubrey" by Bread for her long ago. I wonder if she kept it? "And how I miss the girl, and I would go a thousand times around the world just to be closer to her than to me (Bread)."

One time she wrote me a card, and in it wrote, "I love you, Michael" over 100 times. No one else ever did this before so it's a safe bet she actually loved me. Then I got far too close to her heart so someone told her to break up with me. Apparently, an influential adult thought she was too young at 17 to love me so much. They may have been right. I never truly understood it because she gave me some canned bologna excuses.

Within three weeks, she went from loving me a hundred times to breaking up with me in the stairway of the main hall of LHS. There was a big parrot mural painting on the wall. The parrot did not laugh as tears rolled down my cheeks. She cried too because love hurts sometimes. That parrot is still there but his days may be numbered. They are now talking about building a new High School. I will miss our old High School building when they knock it down but not the sad memory of that parrot.

Phil Collins "Against All Odds" summed up how I felt in early 80's. "How can I just let you walk away? Just let you leave without a trace. When I stand here taking every breath with you. You're the only one who really knew me at all. How can you just walk away from me when all I can do is watch you leave? Because we shared the laughter and the pain. And even shared the tears. You're the only one who really knew me at all... You coming back to me is against all odds, it's the chance I've got to take."

John Waite was singing "Missing You" on the radio, and I was crushed, losing my girl so suddenly. It was heartbreaking to take. The situation was hard to understand and seemed completely unfair, like Noah and Ally in the famous movie *The Notebook*. All I could do was "Wish you the best" like in the famous Lewis Capaldi song. She took off for beautiful Vermont to attend college, and I moved into my Grandmother's attic and studied at Northeastern University in Boston. From there, all I could do is hope for "Better Days" as expressed in the Goo Goo Dolls song.

I ran into this same old girlfriend at Wilson's Farm perhaps twenty-five years later on Christmas Eve as the snow fell. She was doing some last minute shopping for her Family's holiday. We chatted a bit; then she innocently gave me a kiss on the cheek, and I watched her drive away. "Just for a moment I was back in school, and felt that old familiar pain. And as I turned to make my way back home, the snow turned into rain" ("Same Old Lang Syne" by Dan Fogelberg). It really was snowing, then raining on that day at Wilson's Farm in Lexington, and I realized that it was, in fact, what Dan Fogelberg was singing about when he watched his old love drive away.

As a Boston suburb Catholic young teenage man in the late 70's, I had big dreams of attending either the University of Notre Dame or Boston College. I had only seen Notre Dame through football games on TV or through Rudy's eyes in that inspirational movie *Rudy*. I always wore Notre Dame or Boston College gear. In fact, I still regularly wear both schools' sweatshirts and pullover coats

Boston College Chestnut Hill (courtesy of Boston College Alumni Association)

I took the subway, and walked the Boston College campus with my friend Paul "Babs" Babineau in 1979. We had tickets to one of their home football games. Their students, school, and crowd were simply amazing. BC beat Rutgers that day. I fell in love with Boston College; perhaps that's why my father put his foot down.

By 10th grade, my Dad pulled me aside with my mother present and stated: "You're the smartest of our six children but only rich kids go to those fancy colleges and universities. Don't get any big dreams, they are not happening." He further added "You can go to Community College in Bedford by taking a bus there, and go get a job to pay for it." I was 15 and crushed but I was used to it all too well by then. You don't ever get to pick your parents. Accept that, and do your best. That was my plan. I thought to myself no one would stop me.

My older brother Joe and I got lucky and moved into affordable housing in the Old Muzzey School, which was a Massachusetts trend. It was a tiny one-room place but a start for us. Thank heaven we found it even though I mostly slept on a cheap uncomfortable couch. Our friends Asc, Babs, and Kevin "Dools" Dooley would come over all the time. We watched movies, laughed, and were young bachelors.

That changed fast when I met my beautiful Boston College (BC) girl Laurel. Soon I was looking for a bigger condo; and buying a second car, hoping to marry the angel whom God himself sent down from heaven to save me. It had to be God himself because I have never deserved someone as smart, beautiful, kind, and loving as Laurel. I quietly prayed in church thanking God for Laurel coming into my life.

Time passed, and the innocence of our youth has long since left but she shines like a diamond with her heart of gold. My wife is the Queen of Hearts that Don Henley (Eagles) sang about in their "Desperado" song. And so magnificent is the splendor of *Lady Liberty's Treasure Hunt* reflected in her beautiful blue eyes' gaze. That's right Laurel is *Lady Liberty* in this story, and my treasure hunt honors my wife and best friend Laurel.

My Dad and I loved "The Good, The Bad, and The Ugly" western movie. It's about an 1862 Civil War gold treasure buried in a grave. It's a great Clint Eastwood Great movie to watch; but just to be straightforward; *Lady Liberty's Treasure* is not hidden inside of a fenced graveyard or cemetery. Digging inside a fenced cemetery at someone's grave is illegal; please don't ever do that. Enjoy cemeteries for their history but look outside their stonewalls or fences for treasure. Thank you.

Please don't bother my ancestors' graves because you would be wasting your time, and you would only earn their wrath. Knowing my family members; you would end up with the same fate as John Carter, and his compatriots who disturbed Egypt's King Tut's tomb in the Valley of the Kings.

Forrest Fenn original signed picture (Author's collection)

Please take your family and friends on some well-deserved vacations, and enjoy a great United States Northeast States treasure hunt while remembering the past for just a bit. My friend Forrest Fenn would have put on his favorite red coat, and taken a couple of weeks off for a shot at the glory of finding a treasure.

Heritage Auctions Dallas, Texas, sold some of Forrest Fenn's treasure for over 1.2 million dollars in 2023. I was able to purchase numerous items from this collection. Some of these items are out there waiting for treasure hunters to find them. I know another super cool Forrest Fenn treasure hunter Justin Posey. He grew up in Arizona then moved to Texas. He and his wife had a deluxe van. They spent a lot of time hiking and treasure hunting. His LLC acquired Fenn's treasure chest. Justin is a great guy with a really cool collectible! I love his spirit, and so did Forrest Fenn. I'm glad he currently has Forrest Fenn's treasure chest!

So remember and learn from the great treasure hunt searches that have gone on before: *Masquerade* (The Golden Hare), *The Secret*, and *The Thrill of the Chase*. Enjoy their glorious stories and successes but don't make tragic decisions or mistakes that may put your self or others at risk. That would be just foolish; and treasure hunters are required to be clever, wise and safe at all times!

The treasure may be anywhere along these fine routes and places mentioned anywhere in this book, from the front cover to the back cover. Of course, my books are deliberately vague, so it will take effort or luck to find one of my treasures.

The effort will be well worth it when you look with awe upon the treasure. So quit armchair searching for it to death; put on your sneakers or hiking shoes, and go forth and find its secret place if you dare. You are the Captain of your own destiny.

This treasure hunt and chase is extremely difficult but not impossible. It may take a day, week, summer, or some years, who can truly say? If you would like some challenge, and exercise over several days of vacation or maybe more, jump up, get dressed, bring your water bottles, and breathe in the fresh air. Life is so beautiful for those with a positive spirit. Stay young at heart, and you will live long, healthy, and happy lives.

The large crowd smiled as new names were added to the Troop 79 Andover Eagle Scout Board. Matthew, Corey, Drew, and Nate had all done great! With pictures showing much of their 12-year journey, their parents beamed with pride.

I'm hoping that Troop 79 Andover, Massachusetts will eventually decide to change their Troop Flag motto to: "*The Treasure Troop*" because Scouting with them helped inspire my two books. Troop 79 is a Boys (age 11 - 17) Troop that meets during the school year on Thursday evenings at 7 PM at Saint Robert's Parish Driscoll Hall 198 Haggetts Pond Rd Andover, MA 01810. Feel free to come visit us during the school year, if your children may be interested in Scouting. We refer all local young ladies to our sister Troop 73G at South Church 41 Central St. Andover, MA. My contact information is in the front of the book if your family has any questions about Scouting. Here is the Troop 79 Andover, Massachusetts website: andover79.mytroop.us .

Together, we at Troop 79 Andover experienced many great trips, like visiting the USS *Massachusetts*, *Salem*, and *Constitution* ships. Despite the cold air, our hearts were warm with pride. The Scouts explored the awesome Charlestown Museum, and climbed the Bunker Hill where so many met their doom in courageous but foolhardy charges. They marveled at the famous rowboat ride commemorated on a stone marker nearby.

Another time, the Scouts had to earn their Citizenship in the Nation Merit Badges. We parked by Fiske Hill Lexington, near the Bluffs, and embarked on a quiet hike across three towns in pouring rain. A Ranger, dressed in brown on the Lexington Lincoln line, smiled and played a great movie narrated by Mr. Amos Doolittle for our Scouts. It is definitely worth your time to watch that movie in the Minuteman National Park Visitor's Center.

Troop 79 Scouts surely learned to respect all who served in the military. All the young men on this trip later achieved Eagle Scout! Well done. Make our nation and world a better place.

Back to 1775 - Smith, Percy, and crew, who returned to Peirce's Hill for an incredible fight at the Foot of Rocks. Ripley painted this one too, but it's hard to find any of his works from the amazing Worcester American Revolution prints collection. I have many or all of the artworks that I discuss. I have been collecting them for over 30 years.

They fought their way into North Cambridge, but Percy wisely took the Prospect Hill route through present-day Somerville to get to Charlestown Neck and to the safety of the cover of HMS Somerset guns. The British finally reached safety as the sun set after about 40 miles of marching, and fighting in less than 24 hours. The Colonists' long journey for freedom was just beginning. Many miles and battles still lay ahead. General Percy later fought under General Howe at the Battle for Fort Washington in Manhattan, and in the Battle of Long Island in '77.

Battle of Long Island by Dominick D'Andrea (Public Domain)

I visited Long Island with my wife, and family many times. We brought our children to Fire Island Beach. Laurel's grandparents, David and Juliet Burke, had a year-round house at Mastic Beach, NY. Laurel's family visited there a lot. We called her grandfather "Pop." He was a great guy. We took him to Ireland with us around 1992. Sadly, he had lost his beautiful wife, Juliet, around 1980. He told me in Ireland, as we finished his second trip to Ireland, that he had a great trip but only wished Juliet was with him to see Ireland again. That's love. It's the most powerful force in this world under God.

Laurel's Uncle Byron and Aunt Christine Burke live on Long Island. They are the nicest people in the world. They have a son, Danny, who is married to Shannon, named after the famous West Coast Irish River. They also have their amazing daughter Nancy and her husband, New York Deputy Sheriff Will Anderson. We love them all so very much. They are so much fun, especially when their grandchildren Quinn and Kelsey are around.

Byron basically lives on the ocean fishing on his boat every chance he gets for dinner. Byron is close to the treasure; that he seeks, because he is a great fisherman. His daughter Nancy has a lucky, goofy, white cloth fishing cap. She offered it to me for good luck. I declined and stuck to my baseball hat. She put on her lucky hat, caught all the fish, laughed, and said, "See, you should have worn the lucky fishing hat." I caught nothing, and had to admit Nancy was right. Nancy is a great teacher; I should have listened to her advice. Well, I caught no fish, but I enjoyed a great day on Long Island Sound with Byron and his lovely daughter Nancy Burke Anderson.

The Burke's are a great Irish New York family. I proudly wear my Irish-themed Long Ireland Beer Company hat with my 69th NY Irish Regiment Battle Flag tee shirt. It's a copy of the Irish Brigade Flag that President John F. Kennedy gave to the Irish Parliament back in '63. I purchased this cool t-shirt at Irish Green and Union Blue Shop in Gettysburg, Pennsylvania. I love Gettysburg and the Irish Brigade!

After defeating the British in the Siege of Boston on Saint Patrick's Day 1776, General Washington moved his up to 19,000-man Army to defend the Port of New York. The British, under General Howe, brought troops to the Battle of Long Island. Further British ships arrived with Generals Henry Clinton and General Charles Cornwallis. The British brought 8,000 Hessians with them for a total of 32,000 troops, 400 ships including 73 warships.

General Howe, who had the Colonials completely outgunned, offered Washington and all his troops pardons if they surrendered. Washington bravely responded, "Those who have committed no fault want no pardon."

The British attacked Gravesend, Flatbush, and Guan Heights. They won these battles and took Long Island and Manhattan. It was an awful rout and forced Washington to cut through New Jersey into Pennsylvania. Word of Washington's brave words spread across the colonies and helped to inspire all. Though Washington lost 2000 men to the British loss of 388, he still earned the praise of the nation for his conduct. A tough strategic loss but a moral win.

Old Colony House Washington Square (courtesy of Kenneth C. Zirkel)

General Percy then went to the Battle of Portsmouth, Rhode Island, also called Quaker's Hill. The British seized Newport, and the Colonials withdrew. The British occupied Newport from 1776 to 1779. The battle was considered a draw; both sides took relatively small losses. Percy ended up quarreling with General Howe. He resigned his officer's commission and went home to his duties as a Lord. Percy actually won the prize by going back home. Lord Hugh Percy was able to survive the war; and live out his life, unlike many of his compatriots. Newport residents were mostly loyalists but the British Troops interfered with commerce and brought disease. Newport residents preferred no troops there as the British set up soldier's barracks at the Colony House and Trinity Church.

Historic Trinity Church (courtesy of Newport Historical Society)

Colonel Smith also went with General Howe to the Battle of Long Island and then fought in the Battle of Quaker Hill in Newport, Rhode Island, in '78. France joined this battle with its Navy and General Rochambeau's troops as an American ally. Vive La France!

French Army General Rochambeau with French Reenactors (courtesy of RI Historical Society)

Stormy waters damaged British and French ships. The great French US Colonial Major General Marquis de Lafayette led the French troops. This rallied the Rhode Island, Massachusetts, and New Hampshire militia. The Continental Artillery came as well to join the effort. Generals Sullivan and Greene fought off Smith's attack, but the results of the battle were inconclusive.

Lt. General Rochambeau by Charles–Phillippe Larivieve (courtesy of Wikimedia Commons)

On July 11, 1780 French Royal Army Commander in Chief Lt. General Count de Rochambeau arrived in Newport Harbor. It was the King's Beach in the morning but General Rochambeau's beach by nightfall. He set up his Headquarters at the Vernon House. His French Army of 5800 troops, and 6000 sailors anchored in the harbor. The set up their military camp near Wood's Castle in Sachuset close to current Peabody Beach and Third Beach, Middletown. All those Newport beaches are really nice. The French soldiers remained in Newport until June 10, 1781 then marched to Waterman's Tavern near Seven Men's Farms Conventry, and on to Providence. From there, they marched south to join Washington's Army on the Hudson River.

Historic Vernon House 46 Clarke St. (courtesy of Newport Restoration Foundation)

Newport is a historical treasure with all its great history, and beautiful mansions to tour. Newport has a truly great history that even Presidents have enjoyed! Plan a vacation here or visit. It's just breathtaking!

Wedding Bells St. Mary's Church Sept. 12, 1953 (Public Domain)

Newport, Rhode Island was also historically important in the 1950's and 1960's because US Senator John F. Kennedy fell in love with Jacqueline Bouvier who lived at the Hammersmith Farm 225 Harrison Ave by the ocean. The Kennedy family would frequent Newport together for the next 10 years. They were a treasure to our nation; and the world loved, and admired them. The famous Red Sox 7th inning stretch song: "Sweet Caroline" written by Neil Diamond was actually inspired by the Kennedy's, and their daughter Caroline. It really was "Camelot" as song by Fiona Fullerton & Richard Harris.

President John F. Kennedy greeted by his son John at Hammersmith Farm (Public Domain)

President Kennedy enjoyed sailing off the coast of Newport (Public Domain)

The British 10th Regiment of Foot served in America until 1778 and then returned home. Lt. General Smith was given command of the 11th Regiment Devonshire Regiment. Their motto was Semper Fidelis (Always Faithful), just like our US Marine Corps. I wonder if General Smith feared meeting his God after commanding a massacre on Lexington Common in 1775? He died in 1791.

Bennington, Vermont Monument (photograph by Michael O'Connell)

In '77, General John Stark led his New Hampshire Troops from Manchester and Massachusetts Regiments to the Battle of Bennington. They crossed Bennington, Vermont. Bennington was a strategic location with Colonial supplies and munitions. This was the target of the British who marched then encamped close to the border in New York.

General Stark then marched west about 10 miles into New York to Walloomsac, Hoosick to attack the British and Hessian Troops staged there. Stark's Command; was reinforced by Colonel Seth Warner, and the Vermont Green Mountain Boys. Vermont's General Ethan Allen was later at Bennington, too, and had conversations with General Stark.

General John Stark Battle of Bennington, Walloomsac, Hoosick, NY 1777 (Public Domain)

Stark's combined forces met and defeated part of General John Burgoyne's Army under Baum. This was a major strategic victory, capturing 1000 men, and a huge turning point in the war. It was a great achievement for New Hampshire and for the Colonial Army under Washington. Vermont proudly celebrates this day as Bennington Battle Day. Bennington is the closest major town to their actual battle location in New York and was the staging place for the Colonists' great victory that was desperately needed to buoy American resolve.

Brevet Major General William Wells (Public Domain)

Vermont also took great pride in the First Vermont Cavalry, led by General William Wells. They fought in nearly every major battle with the Army of the Potomac from 1861 to 1865. Their beautiful flags are available to see in their Capitol Building basement in Montpelier. You have to visit when their legislature is on break, though, because that's their legislation session break room. I loved visiting their Flag Room.

Major General Hugh Judson Kilpatrick had a bad reputation of getting his troops killed. His nickname from the Troops was "Kill Cavalry" Kilpatrick. General Kilpatrick on his own initiative ordered Brigadier General Elon Farnsworth to charge the Confederate Troops after the repulse of Pickett's Charge by the Union Troops at Gettysburg July 3, 1863. This was an ill advised move because there may have been about 10,450 Confederate Troops here in this general area of the battlefield. It was well known; at the time, that when cavalry charged on horseback against massed infantry it was a reckless or perilous move disregarding the lives of the soldiers under your command.

Farnsworth's Charge at Gettysburg by Don Stivers (Courtesy of donstivers.com)

General Farnsworth and Major William Wells led this gallant cavalry attack at Gettysburg to assist the Union Infantry near Little Roundtop. General Farnsworth was killed in the charge, and Major Wells then led his Cavalry Battalion into combat against the battle tested CSA 4th Alabama Infantry, 9th Georgia Infantry, and 15th Alabama Infantry. General William Wells earned the Congressional Medal of Honor at Gettysburg for his heroic actions leading his cavalry troopers under heavy enemy fire then getting them back to the safety of Union Lines.

The Vermont Infantry Brigade also won the Battle of Cedar Creek, Virginia. There is a huge, beautiful mural in the Vermont State Capitol of this proud victory. The First Vermont Cavalry also helped make Cedar Creek a rout under Generals Sheridan and Custer. William Wells had a brigade in Custer's Division.

There is a beautiful bronze statue of Brevet Major General William Wells at South Confederate Ave where it passes Plum Run in Gettysburg. I stood there and looked in awe at this lifelike sculpture. This is the original sculpture; there is another like it in Burlington, Vermont. It's simply beautiful. There is also a bronze plaque there of the 1st Vermont Cavalry to honor their service, too.

Oct. 19, 1864 CSA Raiders of St. Albans, VT (courtesy of Vermont Historical Society)

Confederate Raiders under CSA Irregular Cavalry Officer Lt. Bennett Young also showed up uninvited at St. Albans, Vermont. They disguised themselves and blended in. Eighteen to twenty-two CSA soldiers came by train from Canada and arrived at Saint Albans train station. Most of these Confederate soldiers had escaped from Union prisons to neutral Canada.

CSA Lt. Bennett Young leads St Albans Vermont Raid (courtesy of St. Albans Museum)

St Albans, VT is a nice city to visit with great amenities (photograph by Michael O'Connell)

The CSA irregular cavalry troops stayed at the American Hotel North Main Street, and St. Albans House Lake St at Catherine St. Both buildings still stand today. They stole horses, held folks hostage, and robbed the St. Albans, Franklin County, and National Banks. They shot a couple of folks, killing a man, and stole more than $200,000 (over 4 million dollars of today's money value), and held folks at gunpoint on their Town Common.

The Old Covered bridge on Bridge St (courtesy of Sheldon Vermont Historical Society)

The uniformed CSA Irregular Cavalry unit rode north 10 miles to Sheldon Bridge and set in on fire. Lt. Young then changed his plan and decided against trying to rob the Sheldon Bank; due to all the commotion in the area, and folks becoming alerted. The war acts of CS Lt. Bennett Young; and his men in St Albans then Sheldon, Vermont were the furthest northern incident of the US Civil War. The residents of Sheldon were alert and put out the fire saving the bridge. Many years later the bridge was swept away by flooding in 1932.

Modern day Sheldon Bridge Vermont 13.5 miles to Canada (photograph by Michael O'Connell)

Capt. George Conger Greenwood Cemetery St Albans VT grave (courtesy of Conger Family)

They then rode 13.5 miles north as the sunset on their stolen horses into Canada near the current Morses Line (circa 1871). A posse was formed and led by a Captain George Conger of the First Vermont Cavalry. They illegally arrested seven CSA soldiers in neutral Canada. The rest got away with the loot for their CSA government and armies supply needs.

Original St. Albans Bank currency images (Author's collection)

Canadian authorities seized the prisoners of war and carefully reviewed the matter, eventually releasing them as soldiers fighting a war, and then giving them back most of the money they stole from the 3 banks they robbed at Saint Albans, Vermont.

I believe the CSA St. Albans Vermont Bank robberies inspired CSA Irregular Cavalry soldier Jesse James, and his brother Frank James to become outlaw bank robbers after the US Civil War had ended. It seems likely to me because this was national news in October 1864, and the James Brothers fought for the Confederate States out of Missouri as irregular cavalry under William Quantrill and Bloody Bill Anderson. Clint Eastwood's amazing movie *The Outlaw Josey Wales* (1976) is about this time period. Another interesting movie about this conflict is called *Ride With The Devil* (1999).

The Outlaw Josey Wales – Clint Eastwood autograph (Author's collection)

I have a document at home that Bennett Young signed later in life. The Southerners referred to him in their writings as General Young for his veteran activities after the war, but he was never made General during the war. I also bought original St. Albans and Franklin County bank currency from before 1864. Interesting collectibles. Saint Albans is well worth the visit. You have to make sure that the St Albans Museum 9 Church St is open; for it is run by volunteers, and has limited hours. Their museum is an absolute treasure, if you like history.

Various Civil War pieces carried by both sides (Author's collection)

Young's efforts to distract Union war efforts in Virginia did not work. Grant kept his march on toward Richmond; and at Lee's Army anywhere it went to cut Grant off, and defend Richmond. A truly sad war 600,000 or more people died during it.

Original Civil War Pieces (Author's collection)

The First Vermont, led by General Wells, was among the greatest of Union Cavalry Regiments, fighting throughout the US Civil War in the hardest-fought campaigns and battles. I have an 1860 Army Colt that was issued to this amazing cavalry unit. I have some cool cavalry swords, too. May the First Vermont Cavalry never be forgotten.

Vermont's Green Mountains are so beautiful, and their residents have always fought hard for Liberty. Ethan Allen led the Green Mountain Boys to Fort Ticonderoga to help Henry Knox to assist in capturing the fort, seize the cannon, and then deliver them to Washington in Cambridge. Washington had these cannons delivered to Dorchester Heights to free Boston. The British had to leave by ship to Nova Scotia, Canada.

General Knox's Noble Train of Artillery dragged by the Oxen (Public domain)

General Henry Knox and his men's actions were brilliant along what is now known as the Henry Knox Trail from New York across Massachusetts. This historic and important trail is well marked across New York and Massachusetts.

Saratoga National Park, New York plaque (courtesy of National Park Service)

My beautiful wife was born in Saratoga Springs, New York. Not far from there, the Battle of Saratoga took place in 1777. General John Burgoyne led an invasion from Canada, hoping to capture the capital of New York at Albany. He was trying to cut off New England from the rest of the American colonies.

Captured at Saratoga British 6 pound cannon (photograph by author)

Burgoyne gained victory in the initial battle, but the Americans then surrounded him with a much larger force at Saratoga under General Horatio Gates. The truly amazing General Daniel Morgan fought here, as did General Benedict Arnold. On October 17, 1777 General Burgoyne surrender his army to General Gates, 18 large bronze artillery pieces, and twelve 6 pound field pieces.

British 2000 pound cannon captured at Saratoga, NY (photo by author)

The Battle of Bennington helped the American cause by capturing a thousand British Troops that were sent to help the British at the Fort. This greatly helped the Provincials to prepare for and capture Fort Ticonderoga and all it's cannon. Burgoyne tried to fight his way out but was forced to surrender at Saratoga, NY. General Daniel Morgan later fought with great acclaim at the Battle of Cowpens in South Carolina in 1781. This was among the great turning points of the war.

Fort Ticoderoga Cannon (Courtesy of Wikimedia Commons Public Domain)

I loved Social Studies and French in Junior HS. Our Social Studies teacher Mr. Cornish told us about his trip to Washington D.C., and did a slide show. In that presentation, he discussed General Lafayette's contributions in the American Revolution; and his 1824 tour to Lexington, MA, NH, VT, ME, NY, CT, RI, NJ and PA among other places. After class, I went immediately to the Clarke School Library and got a book about Lafayette. I then hurried to my French class with Ms. Windsor. The late bell had already rung so I ran then scurried to my assigned front row seat. She walked up to me; and speaking in French, asked why I was late? I held up the book, and simply said I was at the library. She saw Lafayette on the cover, and smiled. I then said "vive la France." She laughed with apparent joy; and I received an A in French, and Social Studies that year. I got an A from Coach Reed in Phys Ed, too. America is still celebrating General Lafayette, and so am I.

Honoring General Lafayette's visited to Lexington, MA 200 years later (photo by author)

When French King Louis XVI learned of Burgoyne's surrender at Fort Ticonderoga and Saratoga, New York he signed a formal Franco-American alliance on December 4, 1777. France realized America had the hope of winning the war. France began sending soldiers, donations, loans, military arms, and supplies. They sent an entire Army and their Navy to trap Cornwallis at Yorktown, Virginia via Newport Rhode Island, helping force British General Lord Charles Corwallis to surrender to General George Washington on October 17, 1781. Vive la France!

Battery Park defended Lake Champlain Burlington, Vermont (photo by author)

During the War of 1812 with Britain the US 11th Infantry (which was recruited from NH and VT) set up a camp at Burlington Vermont. They set up a shore battery to fight off any aggression by the British coming south about 40 miles from the Canadian line on Lake Champlain. This was a wise move because British

Captain Murray after attacking Plattsburg, NY sent a part of his large flotilla against shipping in Burlington Bay. On August 2, 1813 Churchill's Battery at Burlington exchanged cannon fire with the British fleet. This engagement resulted in the British ships withdrawing back to Canadian waters.

Without France, there would be no United States. They saved us. Without the United States, there would be no France. We saved them in WW1 and WW2. The light of Lady Liberty shines brightly in Paris and New York Harbor.

Washington's Pennsylvania Headquarters December 1776 (author's old postcard collection)

General George Washington needed to know the disposition of the British and Hessian Troops General Cornwallis had left to defend New Jersey at Trenton in December 1776. Washington met with Butcher John Honeyman of Armagn County Cavan Ireland. Washington sent Honeyman as a spy to Trenton. Honeyman; who was a well-known trader to the British, spoke with their Commander Colonel Rall and convinced him the Colonials were in no shape to attack him. Honeyman also noted all the dispositions of the Hessian troops, which he reported back to Washington. Honeyman's efforts worked to lull the enemy and Washington decided to launch a surprise attack.

Washington Crossing Historic Park (photograph by Michael O'Connell)

Washington then worked with Irish immigrants Patrick "Paddy" Colvin and Sam McConkey. Colvin was a trusted friend of Captain John Barry, and Washington had him plan the simultaneous ferry crossings of the Troops, supplies, horses, wagon and cannon at Colvin's, and McConkey's Ferries. Future Presidents George Washington, James Madison, and James Munroe crossed here with John Stark, Alexander Hamilton, and Marquis De Lafayette. They may have also used Howell's Ferry and Dunk's Ferry as well in their operations in Pennsylvania and New Jersey December 1776 and January 1777.

Washington Crossing the Delaware by Emanuel Leutze (Public Domain)

The very brave and tactically brilliant General George Washington led his 2400 troops across the Delaware River from Bucks County, Pennsylvania, into New Jersey, starting at 10 PM on Christmas 1776. General Nathanael Green and General John Sullivan served under Washington in the Battle of Trenton on Dec. 26th. Washington surprised and defeated the 1500 Hessian Troops that opposed him. About 1000 Hessian Troops were captured. General Washington shook one of his young officer's hands and said, "This is a glorious day for our country."

Battle of Trenton, NJ Dec. 26, 1776 by H. Charles McBarron Jr. (Public Domain)

Washington took this momentum; and decided to capture Princeton, New Jersey next. Generals Alexander Hamilton and Hugh Mercer assisted Washington and his 4500 men in defeating British Generals Lord Charles Cornwallis, Charles Mawhood, and their 1200 Troops at Princeton. General Mercer died from a mortal wound during this action. Washington repulsed an attack and then circled around General Cornwallis and stole the march on Princeton. Washington then personally led his men to victory. The British were forced to evacuate Central New Jersey.

Estimates are the 1/4 of the Continental Army were Irish by birth or ancestry. British oppression drove them from Ireland, and made them sympathetic to the cause of the American Revolution. Washington became master of New Jersey thanks to a patriotic group of Irishmen: General John Sullivan, Colonel Edward Hand, Captain John Barry, Patrick Colvin, Sam McConkey, John Honeyman, Patrick Lamb, and Irish recruits in his Army. The Irish helped turn the tides of war in New Jersey.

Battle of Princeton, NJ Jan. 3, 1777 by James Peale (Public Domain)

Washington Monument Morristown (Public Domain)

Washington then led his troops to Morristown, New Jersey, for Winter Quarters. The town's location held a strategic advantage for the Colonial Army by being between New York City and Philadelphia.

Washington's Headquarter at the Ford Mansion Morristown, NJ (Public Domain)

The Ford Mansion was General George Washington's Morristown Headquarters December 1779. It's a beautiful place to visit.

Generals Washington, Hamilton & Lafayette in Morristown, NJ 1780 (Public Domain)

The Marquis de Lafayette arrived at Washington's Morristown Headquarters with news that the French would be sending 6000 men led by Count de Rochambeau. Lafayette recalled General Washington's "eyes filled with tears of joy." Washington loved Lafayette like a son.

My son Ryan and I visited the Ford Mansion and a beautiful sculpture of General George Washington at Morristown. I immediately wrote to Mort Kunstler about the place, the events that occurred there, and Mr. Kunstler created a beautiful art print called "Lafayette with Washington at Morristown." You can purchase it on Mort Kunstler's official website. I just love Lafayette's story. He was a truly amazing man and even did a Tour of America later in life. Lafayette's tour is an amazing historical journey in itself worth studying to those who enjoy history. He traveled from NY, RI, CT, Quincy & Lexington, MA, Portsmouth to Cornish, NH, Windsor & Burlington, Vermont and all the way south to Washington D.C. and Virginia in 1826, etc.

Washington & Lafayette at Valley Forge by H.B. Hall 1931 (Public Domain)

During the winter of 1777-1778, Washington and the Continental Army set up their Encampment at Valley Forge, close to Philadelphia in Eastern Pennsylvania. Washington and his Army were eagerly awaiting the French Army and Navy to join their cause. The British had recently captured one of the truly important cradles of Liberty, Philadelphia.

March to Valley Forge Winter Headquarters 1777 -1778 by William Trego (Public Domain)

After the Morristown, New Jersey difficult winter previously, Valley Forge Pennsylvania proved even more challenging for the Continental Army. Nearly 25 percent of Washington's troops died there. They gave all so our nation would have a chance to exist. Never forget their sacrifice for our freedom.

Washington Kneeling in Prayer (courtesy of Freedoms Foundation at Valley Forge)

Myth has it that General Washington went off alone with his horse; to a clearing in the woods where he knelt and prayed in the snow for the Continental Army to survive and be victorious. Arnold Friberg created a famous painting of this moment called "The Prayer at Valley Forge." I love the above sculpture of Washington at Valley Forge, and that art print, too.

Washington's Valley Forge Headquarters (courtesy of National Park Service)

Freedoms Foundation Valley Forge, PA helps thousands of students obtain a greater understanding, and appreciation of American history and civic responsibilities through their many programs. Freedoms Foundation and I share common goals. Please learn more about them at freedomsfoundation.org .

After the American and French victory at Yorktown in October 1781 General Washington strategically moved the Continental Army north to areas around Newburgh, NY. Washington sent General Rochambeau and the French Army back to Newport, RI.

Washington Headquarters by the Hudson River 84 Liberty St. Newburgh, NY (NYHS photo)

Washington sent his 7000 Troops to set up winter camp; with about 500 members of their families, and to train while peace talks occurred in Paris, France. The Troops and some of their families set up camp at New Windsor Cantonment Site.

Training Reenactment at 374 Temple St New Windsor, NY (NY Historic Site Public Domain)

General Washington brought General Henry Knox & General Horatio Gates with him to continue training their troops, and artillery in the event further hostilities broke out with Great Britain. General Knox, and General Gates established their Headquarters nearby at 289 Forge Hill Rd. Vails Gate, NY.

Major General Henry Knox & Major General Horatio Vails Gate, NY HQ (Public Domain)

Sunset at Hasbrouck's House (courtesy of Wikimedia Commons)

Reenactment of Knox's Artillery at Vails Gate, NY (NY Historic Site Public Domain)

I just love New York; it is such a natural, and historic treasure. I'm going to be forced to stop here about halfway through the American Revolution; at the Pennsylvania and New Jersey southern borders. I have only just started getting our readers interested in these great circumstances that began our American Revolution. The American Revolution, War of 1812 and US Civil War were heavily fought in the Southern States but that would be make the book way too long, and the treasure search area far too great.

I have also just lightly touched on the US Civil War. But I hope to have spurred your interest in these great historic places or events. Remember, today will become history by tomorrow. We are all part of history. Our children, nieces, nephews, or grandchildren are our legacy. They are the future. Teach them wisely, and then let them lead the way.

I am also writing a young adults reader (ages 11 to 17) treasure book without too many adult themes of loss in the writing. This book is called *Riley's Treasure Chase* so youth may go treasure hunting with their families and friends. Riley is my adorable Cavapoo dog. I bet you can guess who the pirate is in the story? I hope *Riley's Treasure Hunt* or *Chase* is a fun adventure for your children, grandchildren, nieces, or nephews to do with their parents, adults or youth groups.

Further, I may complete a follow-up work for about the Southern States not currently included in this Treasure Hunt. I love the South I just could not fit all of that important history into *Lady Liberty's Chase*. I ask parents to please use their discretion; and feel free to skip paragraphs or paraphrase in this current work if they decide to read parts of it to their young children. We all lose folks we love, and I honor and remember my loved ones in this work.

As adults, we have all dealt with illness, disappointments, and loss in our lives. We try our very best as parents to limit these difficult parts of life from our children. That is why I consider this work to be Parental Guidance 13 (PG-13). In short, this book and Treasure Hunt or Chase is more appropriate for Scouts rather than younger Cub Scouts. Thank you for your understanding, and help with this.

The treasure chests may reside in any New England State, New York, New Jersey, or Pennsylvania. All of these states are in play. Anywhere else is out of bounds. So stick to your guns, and don't give up easily. The treasure awaits you from its earthly resting place. It's hidden very well, and my two treasure chases well exceed $100,000 US dollars by 2024 values. I earned all that treasure by getting paid an hourly rate. So it's a big treasure for a person of my means and background. Over time, *Lady Liberty's* treasure may double in value as other treasures' values have done at auction.

Forrest's Fenn's treasure was more valuable because he was a multimillionaire. Heritage Auctions in Texas auctioned off most of Forrest Fenn's treasure for about 1.2 million dollars. The true purchase value of his treasure may have been around $600,000. It perhaps doubled in value over time because maybe 300,000 folks searched for his treasure for almost 10 years. I was one of the Forrest Fenn treasure searchers. I enjoyed Forrest Fenn's *Thrill of the Chase*, and the community of treasure searchers. They are mostly a fun group with a few Indiana Jones and Yosemite Sam types mixed in there a bit. This last sentence just made me laugh.

That level of interest in the Forrest Fenn treasure definitely increased the celebrity value of a cool treasure hunt. I hope my two treasure hunts lasts some years too, and do not have disappointing endings like the United Kingdom's "*Golden Hare*" treasure hunt, and some parts of Forrest Fenn's "*Chase*". Most or all of these problems; were caused by treasure searcher's behaviors, and not their creators.

Please encourage your friends and family to join in this treasure hunt via social media or personal persuasion. They should please consider buying their own books. If you're serious about this or any treasure hunt buy at least 2 copies of the book. Keep one pristine at home for your review. Make the other book your working copy for your treasure hunting notes, etc. Please try to make this an amazing treasure hunt for all!

Somewhere along these unique and special trails is where *Lady Liberty's* treasures lie. So answer the call, and march on until you secure victory. There are clues and hints in the book to help you but it is very difficult though not impossible. It may take you multiple trips to many different places to find a treasure from *Lady Liberty's Treasure Hunt*.

She is my beautiful bride. We married on that August day; in my Family's, St Brigid's Parish Lexington back to 1840. The Princess Bride arrived in a horse and carriage. Flanked by her parents Barbara and David, she gracefully walked down the aisle. Another more beautiful bride never existed. The Angels looked down, cried tears, and clapped with thunder, as Saint Brigid's Parish shook. With tears of joy in her eyes on August 11, 1990, she said, "I do." As she kissed the frog, he became a Prince among men.

She is the greatest of loves and the rarest of jewels, so her *Treasure Hunt* deserves your kindest regards. She was my Princess, and I was her Prince. We matured and I became the "Lord or King of the North" and she became "*Lady Liberty*." Her treasure awaits you; out there until it is found or for all time.

Be safe, wise, kind, and patient and time will always be on your side. No dying or getting hurt is ever a part of this *Chase* or *Treasure Hunt*. The treasure is not inside a fenced cemetery, cave, or any dangerous place.

Please stay out of the water, no wading or swimming is required, don't take unnecessary risks, and no searching please during winter conditions. Don't destroy anyone's property, and please don't annoy or offend others on social media, youtube or blogs.

This *Treasure Hunt* or *Chase* is about fun, not about seeking wealth. I'm not a wealthy person. I privately funded, and solely created this whole venture with my wife's approval. I have made arrangements for my treasure hunts to last for generations; even if I pass this vale, and join all those who left before me.

Anyone who participates waives any right to civil suit against the author of this *Chase*, treasure hunt, his family, friends, business, publisher, or LLC. Buying a book does not create any type of contract with the seller of the book, author, LLC, or any heir or family member to a buyer of any book or product. No treasure hunters or normal people like those folks; so please do not participate in this treasure hunt or chase if you are inclined to civil suit others, or be a sore sport. There was way too much of that stuff after Forrest Fenn's treasure hunt ended. That made Forrest Fenn sad, and me, too.

I am repeating this on purpose. There is no winter searching or swimming or wading across rivers allowed in this *Chase* or *Treasure Hunt* for safety and common sense reasons. Too many folks died during Forrest Fenn's Chase. That's just tragic, and is not allowed in my *Treasure Hunts*. Thank you for following common sense, and safe practices.

More writings, clues, hints, maps, posters or books may follow if no one finds *Lady Liberty's Treasure Hunt* or *Riley's Treasure Chase* treasure chests but I can make no promises or guarantees. We will have to see how things progress.

Please respect *Lady Liberty's Treasure Hunt* and have good old-fashioned family fun in the Spring showers, Summer flowers, or Autumn colors. Stay home when the cold of Winter arrives. I am repeating this on purpose. Winter searching is prohibited so no one perishes or gets injured from the cold weather or conditions.

Life is truly so beautiful, but fleeting. Tell all those you know to please buy a book and get out there searching. As Bob Seger sang so beautifully, "we are older now, but still running against the wind..."

Get the family ready, make travel plans, top off your water bottles, put sandwiches and snacks in your backpack, jump in the car, put on your sunglasses, roll down the windows, crank up the music, play "Boys of Summer" by Don Henley, "Running up that Hill" by Kate Bush, "Solsbury Hill" by Peter Gabriel, "Roll with the Changes" by REO Speedwagon, and Simon and Garfunkel' "America."

When it comes to choosing whether to join in *Lady Liberty's Treasure Hunt* with your family or friends, "I Hope you Dance" with the great inspiration of LeAnn Womack's amazingly, beautiful song.

Now head out for some majorly cool treasure hunting in the great Northeast of the United States of America. "It's something unpredictable, but in the end, it's right, I hope you have the time of your life (Green Day)."

In 2023, an Idaho woman made three trips to Utah and found a $25,000 treasure chest that had been hidden for only seven weeks. Another searcher found a $25,000 treasure in Utah in about a month. I congratulate them; they found a pirate's treasure. I really hope I can do a better job hiding *Lady Liberty's Treasure* and *Riley's Treasure*, too. I fully know that it is really difficult or impossible to predict when a treasure will be located. That is in the hands of the searchers, whom I believe are really smart, and outside my personal control.

There are resources that can help you on this quest, including but not limited to: local libraries, historical societies, "History Traveler" and "American Battlefield Trust" YouTube.com videos, Waze driving or Google Maps driving directions, and anything I mentioned in these "rants and rumblings (Forrest Fenn)." This whole book reflects my life, important historical events, those that influenced me, and those I loved.

Please forgive my deliberately choppy writing style. I wrote this book a paragraph at a time as the moments struck me. I deliberately did not write the book in chronological order. I wrote this book; like a spider builds it's web, one historical string at a time. You will have to figure out which way to go; so you don't get stuck in my web. Also; by bouncing back and forth in time, it's more challenging for you searchers to find the treasure. Hopefully, that way everyone has time to enjoy *Lady Liberty's Treasure Chase*.

I even wrote this book daily on my tablet as my whole family traveled on vacation through Massachusetts, Connecticut, New York, New Jersey, Pennsylvania all the way south to beautiful Hilton Head, South Carolina, for a Burke Family vacation in August 2023. On the way back home, we visited Adams and Bucks Counties in Pennsylvania. Very pretty places; with old, cool historic bridges. Then we bought some great corn in Windsor and stopped at a great New York-style: Rein's Deli at Vernon, Connecticut. Then we made our way back home.

Laurel and her amazing parents at a North Shore springtime garden (photo by Author)

My parents-in-law, David and Barbara Burke, hosted everyone that could come. They are the very best parents and Grandparents to all of their family. We are so lucky to have them in our lives. Dave and Barbara raised five children and ten grandchildren. That's their treasure - family.

Barbara and Dave have been married for over 60 years, overcoming all of life's hurdles, and providing such a great example for all of us to follow. My father-in-law did a slide presentation of our many family trips to Hilton Head showing their grandchildren growing from babies to adults. He then read an email about his and Barbara's generation. Apparently, 99 percent of their age group have already gone, so they are in the top one percent. They remain healthy, vigorous and keep going strong. May we all try to do as well in life. Time with those you love is the greatest treasure of all.

We all love Hilton Head Island for morning coffee, listening to the ocean on the deck, reading, working or writing, beach walking, pools, hot tubs, palm trees, nature, golf, bike riding, and shopping. My wife Laurel, son Brendan, and I just did a bike ride to Sea Pines. We saw two alligators, rode through Sea Pines trails, and then back up the white sands beach, passing the reeds and dunes along the coast with the wind at our backs. That type of serenity is special. As I write this James Taylor's "going to Carolina' is softly playing.

"Men and women are haunted by the vastness of eternity. And so we ask ourselves, will our actions echo across the centuries? Will strangers hear our names long after we are gone, and wonder who we were, how we lived, and how fiercely we loved? (*Troy* movie 2004)." Perhaps my books will outlast our time here as well, and become a reflection of yesterday?

It's not a great poem but perhaps a riddle. There are 9 treasure states; when you multiply that number times two searchers it should be a joy trying to locate a worthy treasure. This is about fun, recreation, and the glory of a journey. If you're only interested in money, perhaps pursue a different folly.

Like any great pirates or privateer's lore from our past, it may be embellished a bit. My treasure books will be no different than pirate treasure stories or privateer tales about Captain Kidd, Black Beard, John Paul Jones, or John Glover. One man's pirate is another person's hero. The British viewed Jones and Glover as villains. US history admires them both. Hopefully, history will remember us all fondly in due time.

Forrest Fenn had his Dad Marvin, older brother Skippy, Yellowstone Park, nine-mile hole, and his nine clues. I had my dad Joseph, my brothers Joe, Paul, and John, all our friends, our fishing spots, sledding & skating places, old schools, sports parks & fields, basketball courts, old trains chugging on by, conservation or recreational lands for hiking & biking, Minuteman Park, 9 states, and about a dozen roads leading to a single town.

The 18th century is worthy of your time but I think I would study the 1800's, too. Sam Adams, Jonas Clarke, and the warning riders all met in secret to hide their treasure caches from future British actions. Some of these warning riders became immortal; others were forgotten or gave their mortal lives to the cause. Coburn tried to remember them all, and so do I.

Percy was wiser and a better leader than Smith or Pitcairn. He was fortunate to return home, and live free without dying. Stark did just as well, and even got a monument or two in his honor.

The farmers gave raise to our National Guard. At a minute's notice they set about but please don't forget the importance of the militia, and Washington's Continental Army. He sent Knox from his Headquarters to bring him the guns from Ticonderoga. Their path was forged with immortal glory.

The Irish were there when Washington had need. Later, they also proved their worth to Meade.

The Moon rose over the west-facing field. The enemy or the patriots marched on past; and paid it no heed but the Sentinel still guards the gate.

LADY LIBERTY'S TREASURE HUNT

Why must you go among the towering Oak and Pine trees? To smell their scent in the summer winds under the cover of night skies. Be careful not to stub your foot on a rock while searching quietly in the dark.

My birth and the birth of our nation were in essentially the same places so my family and friends may have already been there before you. Some have crossed over the river first but we should not forget them. When you study history; you may learn that folks could be right or wrong at the same time, even when they spent time at the taverns.

Sometimes I have felt like I was basically standing in two places at the same time. Is that the present or the past or some line on a map?

If you are fishing by an Old Bridge under the moonlight, beware of the ghosts or you will soon take flight in fear as Crane did.

Remembering America and following the Spirits of '76 may help you find your way to the barns and bridges of yesterday. It has been said that there are ninety-two ways to kill a cat but that will not help you catch a rat. So please leave the mosquitoes to the bats for spraying pests just kills our pollinators. We need the butterflies and the bees or we will all cross the rock walls and fences to rest in cemeteries.

As the weather affects the farmer's field so does each of us that traveled here. Some led, some followed, some bled, yet all mattered.

When my brother Joe hears your group is going treasure hunting, he will proudly exclaim: "Let's go!"

My kid brother John would say to take your mountain bike or go for a hike. My Dad and Aunt Marion would recommend a country drive. My beautiful Irish mother would say look for the rainbow and the treasure after the rain stops.

My brother Paul would say: "smile for it will take a while." My sister Paula would say "if you're not having fun you're doing something wrong." My sister Mary Ann would tell you it's best to have a plan, cell phone, compass, camera, and not to go it alone.

My best friend Kevin Dooley from 60 Taft Ave would say, "moss does not grow on a rolling stone." Paul Babineau from 38 Hibbert Street Arlington would say: take your best shot.

My Sylvia Street neighbor Mike Ascolese would say to head toward Sutherland Park and swing for the fences.

Lucky Coyne from 5 Hibbert St would say enjoy the ride but don't make too many Tavern stops. So no one falls off the horse as it follows April's west winds every year.

My very musical friend Tony Nichols from Chase Ave would say: "you can go your own way. (Fleetwood Mac)" My friend Mark Hedtler from Oak St would say life is too short so enjoy the scenic view.

My athletic friend Barry Neal from Spencer St would advise you to keep moving; and to never, ever quit. Our pal Chris Fuery from Mass Ave at Pleasant St would say it is there in spirit.

My wife and love of my life, Laurel, would advise you to watch out for the snapping turtles, snakes and she greatly hopes you all will "be kind."

My son Brendan would say "non sibi" not for self but others. My daughter would say don't forget to enjoy winter sports. My son Ryan would say: listen to tunes, read good books, and tutor and mentor the young. My youngest son Corey would remind all of you to remember of the importance of community service; and to support all our Public Safety Officials, and all our Scouts across this great nation.

My father-in-law David would say please support and remember all those actively serving our nation in the military, veterans, and to have a good treasure hunt. My mother-in-law Barbara would say to love your family and spend fun times with them.

As for all my wife's siblings, David and Patty would advise you to travel when you can. Chris and Monique would say smile and laugh once again. Michael and Maura would say to enjoy New York, Connecticut, Vermont, and Maine. Brian and Renee would take their plane to Newport in the smallest state in the Union; then head for New Jersey, Pennsylvania, then back over New York across the Berkshires, then to home, sweet home.

Monique's parents Henry and Theresa would ask you to visit the old cemeteries, historical homes, town commons, historical places, and monuments because this is one way to keep history alive and remember the past.

My friends Steve and Christine would say not to forget their beloved New Hampshire. Remember Bartlett is a bit biased because his ancestor was a Founding Father. Kingston's son Dr. Josiah Bartlett signed the Declaration of Independence and greeted General Stark and his soldiers after the Battle of Bennington. A neat ancestor for certain from the "Live Free or Die" state.

Their siblings Catherine and Ron would say to make the April 19th March from Acton and Boxborough to Concord each year, then chase the Redcoats back to Boston. Many other Minutemen Units may complain if you don't do their Town's line of march for their fair share of the fame of that glorious day. Their parents George and Ann would say to keep the faith, and never stop searching for joy.

For me, I would say to pray for the Blue and Gray so they may rest in peace, and not keep haunting us. Respect the sacrifices of the King's Troops but honor the US Colonial Troops, Minutemen and Militia who stood against the world's greatest army 1775 to 1783. Follow each side's footsteps; and pray for all their souls, for God forgives & loves them all and knows best.

If you get thirsty while traveling southeast, remember that the Troops once drank from the mighty Housatonic. Be wise and don't drown in the Long Island Sound.

Remember, the Irish were "Wild Geese," born Celtic warriors who fought for many great armies. It wasn't always a choice but a birthright.

As the saying goes, it's not the treasures we find in life but the journey itself. For a treasure hunt to be fulfilling, it must challenge those brave enough to pursue it.

Whether or not you find my treasure is in Providence's hands. Be brave, and you will achieve greatness.

My Dad used to say, "Stand and take your knocks; if you get knocked down, get back up." We all fall in life; it's what you do when you get back up that matters. Stick to your guns and carry on.

The Prodigal son, the Prince that was promised, or a devilish Pirate or Privateer may aid or deceive you on your journey. It's more fun to be challenged than to win easily. No complaints should be heard in *Lady Liberty's Treasure Hunt* or *Riley's Treasure Chase* because our better nature has no time for that kind of stuff.

This tale is about yesterday, and it belongs to the ages. I hope you and your loved ones enjoy the birds, butterflies, turtles, and flowers along the historic trails, sidewalks, or roads of yesteryear.

How long this treasure hunt lasts, is up to all of you. By joining this quest, each of you becomes part of history, too. Enjoy your adventures.

I went alone or with my *Riley* dog, like a cagey Pirate, and hid a combined treasure over $100,000 in *Riley's Treasure Chase* and *Lady Liberty's Treasure Hunt*. The Pirate made his mark on the world, and perhaps time will remember him for it.

Henry David Thoreau wrote: "I went to the woods because I wished to live deliberately, to confront only the essential facts of life, and see if I could learn what it had to teach, and not, when I came to die, discover that I had not lived."

So, find time to get out there, be brave in the woods, trails, and live, laugh, and love like there is no tomorrow.

Thoreau, Longfellow, Lafayette, and Washington all visited and dined at the Wayside Inn Tavern Sudbury, Massachusetts. So did my dear relatives Aunt Ann & Uncle Tom Beatty, Aunt Maire Cloherty, and my beautiful wife Laurel.

For Thoreau, all roads led to Concord, where he was born, traveled, lived, and died. There's year-round beauty in that special place for all to enjoy. Thoreau was on to something when he said: "That government is best which governs least." He praised Captain John Brown in 1859, and soon after, Union Armies marched singing Brown's name.

Frost certainly overcame a lot of challenges in his life. I wonder if his apples grew better in New Hampshire or Vermont? Perhaps he enjoyed Vermont Maple Syrup more than the New Hampshire brand or not? I think it was great that Robert Frost read a poem for JFK's in Inauguration Day but it's truly sad that neither man made it beyond '63.

John Glover, John Stark, Henry Knox, Harry Lee, Daniel Morgan, Nathanael Greene, Marquis de Lafayette, Count de Rochambeau were all ready when General George Washington called upon them.

Follow the trails of each side's soldiers, warning riders, and their leaders. Where did they start, which direction did they take, where did they fight, and where did it end their journeys?

If all the British soldiers facing you all look the same, you've either hiked or biked too little or too far.

They knew they had walked too far when they saw the flag unfurled.

Remember, as Forrest Fenn once said, it is *Too Far To Walk*." You need a car, bike rack, mountain bikes, comfortable sneakers or hiking shoes, bug spray, sunglasses, and water for my chases, too.

If you see a river, creek, stream, pond, or lake, enjoy the scenery and remember those who fought for freedom or built this country. You may leave your paddles at home, but feel free to safely enjoy kayaking or canoeing safely or swimming on your own but it is not part of my treasure chases. As Forrest Fenn once said: "There'll be no paddle up your creek" but please feel free to fish.

Eric Sloane would wish you a nostalgic summer traveling in Vermont, New Hampshire, Massachusetts Berkshires, New York, Connecticut, or Pennsylvania, seeking America's scenic beauty, barns, and historic covered bridges.

The Spirits of '76 will guide you. If you're near any historical site or General's Headquarters, National, State, City, or Town historical point, or home please visit and enjoy a tour.

It's a safe bet I've already been there because I love those events or have been there on Scouting trips. Please support these historical places; they need visitors, fees, and shop sales to keep teaching history to future generations.

Current borders and rules do not define birds or a Pirate's journey; don't let them define your quest, or you'll return empty-handed.

The treasure may be worth more when found. Forrest Fenn's treasure doubled in value over a decade, proven by a Heritage public auction in Texas. The British Golden Hare treasure sold for an exuberant amount, too. Time will tell what this treasure is worth.

I've said it before, and I'll say it again: the true treasure is spending time with family and friends.

There's no need to go it alone like Thoreau in Walden's Wood. Better to be with others. Even Thoreau himself ended up closer to his family home.

People have asked me to mark an X on the map, but I declined, saying: "like Forrest Fenn's *The Thrill of the Chase*, it's there in spirit."

If you find my treasures, you'll understand why. Forrest was so much fun; I really miss him. That's why I mention him so much. There's a part of him in this quest, and a part of me, too. I remembered many others as well because they are all important to me.

My Grandmother Mary Ann (Doherty) O'Connell was the wisest person I ever met. She would say, "Follow the birds in life; they will show you the way. They sing at night when it's time to sleep and at sunrise when it's time to start your day." Follow the birds, and you will always find your way. She loved Cardinals, and so do I.

My great Aunt Susan Doherty from Strabane Northern Ireland would say to remember the Irish contributions to the birth of the United States, and in defending it.

My beautiful Aunt Maire Ann Cloherty took me to Ireland to live on my Grandparent's Lettercallow, Lettermore County Galway Farm for the summer of 1972. She said: "Michael, your heart is free; have the courage to follow it." I chased rainbows across the stonewalls and fields of Connemara but never found the Leprechaun or his treasure. You have a much better chance now just before the 250th Celebrations start. There's a piece of Connemara in the treasure to honor my Irish ancestors.

I didn't understand my Aunt Maire's Irish proverb at 9, but now at 60, I do. As we grow in life, we age like fine wine. Let the bagpipes play "The Gael" (*The Last of the Mohicans* movie theme) forevermore to remember those who have gone before us. My treasure hunts remember yesterday, and today. I hope you have a great tomorrow searching for them.

As I wrote this, I listened to a Robin sing and heard tranquil waters flow under a covered bridge. Neither minded me joining them for a bit. Please take time to enjoy nature and "Remember America," even if it's just a coffee or lunch break in your busy day.

Wyeth called him a "treasure of Americana." So "I've come to look for America… They have all come to look for America…" as Simon and Garfunkel sang so well.

Our history is also in our infrastructure; take time to enjoy it along your route. Listen to the church bells ring every Sunday morning or on the 4th of July to honor Mr. Northeast.

Two is company, but three is a crowd, considering those state names traveled upon by great men of the past.

The Wood Thrush and Blue Hen may protest as the American Goldfinch beats them to a worm and flies Northeast. The Grouse takes flight as Eagles look down with delight.

Steven Spielberg, Indiana Jones, Byron Preiss, Forrest Fenn, Eric Sloane, Amos Doolittle, Aiden Lasell

Ripley, Nicholas Cage, Dan Brown, and Tom Hanks will be proud of you for seeking the treasure and searching for America. They inspired me with their arts, and I hope they motivate you, too.

One side fought to keep the Crown upon the land; their opponents cried, "don't tread on us," preferring to "live free or die."

Lafayette was like a son to George Washington, admired even more than James Munroe, John Stark, Alexander Hamilton, James Madison, and Henry Knox. Knox got a Fort and Headquarters named after him; Lafayette did a great tour across the Northeast. He was a hero of two nations, honored near the White House.

Indiana Jones knows how to respect the past; as shown in *The Last Crusade* movie, where Harrison Ford was searching for the Holy Grail. That treasure-hunting movie is among my favorites especially the scene in the old church.

Nicholas Cage had great spirit to in his *National Treasure* movie but I don't know anyone named Charlotte. So the secret does not lie there.

We can never know how many days we have, so love those around you like there's no Tomorrow. Be passionate, wise, discreet, thoughtful, and kind in your pursuit of the prize, wherever you are.

It's how we overcome struggles that define us. The same is true for our nation. By overcoming its struggles, a nation lit the lanterns, and *Lady Liberty's* torch.

Lady Liberty knows that the eyes of America, Canada, and Europe are upon us as we all play our part in this treasure hunt. The history of the United States is tied to England, France, Canada, Ireland, Spain and the Netherlands. This treasure hunt respects those nations' contributions to forming the United States of America in its early years. Our history belongs to them too so I hope they join in this treasure hunt for fun.

Stow and Pass rang their bell for Liberty. They gathered at Carpenter's Hall and signed the document for Liberty's sake, calling all nations to light the torch of Liberty.

One campaign may help but you can't win a war in a day or find *Lady Liberty's* treasures without effort.

My Father Joe used to say that pure Copper divining or dowsing rods might help find treasures. Perhaps he was right. He found a British grave at the Bluff's in Lexington in 1973. Him and I led a National Park Ranger to the site now there is a British gravestone there. The Ranger knows where the treasure is but clearly won't tell you.

My mother Brigid told me; as a young child, that the secret toward marching to your goals in life was to following the lucky Irish shamrock. I questioned what does that mean? She responded with her thick Irish accent: "You must follow the three's because they represent the Holy Trinity: the Father, the Son, and the Holy Spirit." She meant it.

Leave no trace behind. A palindrome may help or not, but who's to say?

Visit the Old North Bridge, Acton Common, or Lexington Common, but all that remains there are fallen soldiers, plaques, and hallowed ground. Please don't damage these places. They should look like you were never there. Clean up others folks litter, too. Preserve our public spaces and world for future generations. Thank you.

Seize the moment. Listen to music, hear the birds, smell the flowers, and feel the sun shine brightly upon your face. If it rains, bring an umbrella and a raincoat.

Picture the old trains passing by, the Boston and Maine through Arlington Center on the Minuteman

Bikeway, Arlington Heights, Adams School Pond, East Lexington, Lexington Center, Bedford Depot & Narrow Gauge trail, the Reformatory Line across Bedford to Monument St near the Old Manse and Old North Bridge in Concord, Bruce Freeman Rail Trail from Chelmsford Center, Carlisle, Westford, Acton, Concord to Concord Rd. Sudbury & beyond (still under construction to Framingham). These are all nice mountain biking or hiking trails to enjoy nature, birdsong, exercise, and fresh air. It is wise to use maps to avoid getting lost. Some of these are long rides or walks; so best to split it up, if you don't exercise frequently.

Hike or bike summer trails, sled with your children, skate, ski or snowshoe in winter, or take an autumn or spring drive with hot coffee or hot chocolate and definitely have the radio on.

Time always wins; remember yesteryear but live in the moment, the hour, and the day. Heavy loads will guide you. Haste makes waste. Take your time and do it right.

Enjoy the fragrance of Purple Lilacs, and Rhododendrons in spring. My mother Brigid loved them dearly. My mother in law Barbara loves the Hydrangeas, and the summer gardens.

Monuments remember people who fell or fought bravely but they never shed a tear. It's for us to remember and weep for them.

"It's a nice place for a picnic," says your wife but bring bug spray just in case. The Bats eat the mosquitoes, and the Owl eats the Bats. Both have nesting boxes near the farm. The Pheasant is nearby but wary of the Fisher Cat in the wood.

They named a lake after him but he still lost the war. The actions at the Boston and Lexington massacres are forever attached to their names. Rulers must rule but being righteous is preferable to being cruel.

Chelmsford's Caesar Robbins was righteous and brave; trekking from Chelmsford to fight against the French, then the British. After the skirmish at the rude bridge, Robbins and the Minutemen flanked the British as they marched back toward Lincoln and Lexington.

Their crimson cavalry flag was there in the French and Indian War, the American Revolution, and is a town's pride today. Visit on Patriot's Day weekend to see it at their library. They climb their Liberty Pole every year two weeks before Patriot's Day.

The Mohawk guards her two gates, and the Black-Capped Chickadee sings. And the Moon rose over an open field as the Oak trees bowed.

The Grouse set off from the Mountain Laurel bush to seek its breakfast. The Goldfinch captured its prey among the blue violets.

Two Eagles look across from their perch at the glory of it all.

The state of Delaware is not in play, nor is our Capital in Washington D.C. but please see the spring Cherry Blossoms when you can.

The shadow of the gun marks your way. The Somerset looms great as Pitcairn, Smith, and Percy with his guns prepare to march westward from Lechmere Point's marshland on the Charles River or across the Great Bridge westerly.

The route is set in time, theirs, not yours. A timeline of the French and Indian War, the American Revolution, and the US Civil War may help you understand history and aid you.

Prescott rode with the alarm, noting the farmer's Oxen may be useful later to cross two states. First on a trek with Mary Hartwell to Lincoln Burial ground, then as the Eastern Bluebird sang, on a grander plan to free Boston. He then sent his brother out into harm's way.

"First in peace, first in war, and first in the hearts of his countrymen." These were not mere words but an accurate statement of the bold attack. Marblehead's 14th Continental Regiment, and their Irish compatriots can attest to this acclaim.

Washington and Pleasanton's cavalry fought with ferocity and honor for freedom's cry under US colors.

Their sons fought over what their fathers had won. Ironic and sad.

The Irish fought with Washington and Hancock, helping make America the home of the free and brave. But ads in the Boston Globe in the 1920s still said: "No Irish need apply." This was truly sad for my Irish Grandparents.

Davis and Buttrick would smile on their courage and your treasure hunt "remembering America."

Acton led the vanguard because they had bayonets. "I have not a man afraid to go," he said.

They crossed their arms with honor and courage, bayonets affixed. Wearing Red or Gray, they stood no chance on those celebrated American battle days.

Bedford, Westford, and Lincoln were right there, giving chase as the foe fled east. Woburn, North Reading, Chelmsford, Billerica, Wilmington, Sudbury, and Framingham converged as well.

Behind boulders and trees, they fired upon the column like angry bees, learning well from the French and Indian War how to fight. Fire at the red column, retreat, reload, wait in ambush again, and again. 17 miles is a long way to walk back under fire all day.

Some Irish wore red that day, whether they wanted to or not. Many would never see Ireland again.

The Patriot's flag unfurled near the Bloody Angle; and they gave the last full measure of devotion for liberty, and their young nation. Keep the spirits of '76 alive in your hearts.

The wild geese feed on the open farmlands where the sunflowers smile. Wilson, Thompson and Wyman were there but gone too soon.

Armistead fell four score and seven years later. Hancock said no officer was ever braver. Hancock shed tears for his great friend. Both fell on the same field but Winfield carried on well throughout his life. Five stars will guide you.

The bridge to and from Fairfield was busy in the Summer of '63. The Blue 1st Corps and Gray 1st Corps passed through within four days. One man lost his life; the other beheld the saddest sight of all and was forced to retreat. Ghosts in blue or gray still tell their story today.

The great battle shook the Cumberland but Freedom's cry was heard. President Lincoln's Gettysburg Address echoes across time louder than the cannon fire.

How can such a beautiful place be haunted by executed deserters? Strange circumstances; they wore gray, then blue. Their ghosts remain.

They proudly exclaimed, "live free or die," and "they had not yet begun to fight."

Daring charges on July 2nd & July 3rd on the same battlefield earned them the Medal of Honor and monuments to their bravery. Vermont and Maine were proud of their great achievements.

His blood marks the spot forevermore. Losing a friend is always sad but part of life. Hancock knew this, and so do I.

Their brothers who mourn them never forget the boys from Adams.

The Tower casts a long shadow. Confederate deserters dressed in Union blue soon met the gallows. The last thing they heard was the birdsong of a Ruffed Grouse.

Too bad they are gone now and can't look back on yesteryear.

They dragged heavy loads here to free a city from tyranny. Robbins and Acton were there on Dorchester Heights.

The Troops marched on. You can still hear echoes of musketry or cannon fire.

Claremont and Tasker smiled as the Mountain looked down.

The French and Indian War, American Revolution, and US Civil War are in play. These wars were not civil at all but their valor is remembered.

Washington's adopted son honored New Hampshire, Vermont, Massachusetts and Connecticut. He was a gift to our nation forevermore.

A pirate wanders on, like a swashbuckling privateer, to each state abutting a sea, large lake, or river within the outlined area.

A pirate fears no man, ropes, stonewalls, gates, or property lines. The pirate knows we all die eventually; we have no time to waste so if you are able, get to it.

Some Eagle Scouts or Assistant Scoutmasters may help you learn through Citizenship in the Nation merit badge. Others would say, "let's hike, bike, ski, sled, or enjoy the day."

Try not to be a juvenile delinquent. Pick up your trash and clean up after your dog.

Trains have whistled since the 1800s when they passed the mighty Merrimack. The Pheasant lives nearby and can attest.

The narrow rail use to pass on by so long ago. The Veteran's look back on their bravery, and hope we don't ever forget their need. My Grandfather, father, and uncles were among them.

Presidents and great people have passed many of these hallowed grounds, many times on the campaign trail, or on a journey of remembrance. Now you have joined them.

Take the wayside route across mills, farms, and scenic or historic trails if you hope to get there quickly.

The English "Golden Hare" Chase has nothing on *Lady Liberty's Treasure Hunt* or *Riley's Treasure Chase*. I invite those in Canada, England, Scotland, Ireland, Wales, France, Netherlands, Spain and the rest of the world to prove me wrong. Our history is yours too, so enjoy the treasure hunt. The valuable treasure coins specifically match many countries to honor them. Our history is your history, too.

If you find the right spot where the Purple Finch sings, their souls will approve. Find the large rock near where they rest, sit, pray, and contemplate.

See their farm and blooming flowers too. Seven large steps are before you; so don't trip.

Our wives or mothers always show us the right way. It's best to follow their directions.

Rest on the granite, then head for the cattails and ferns within sight of the beautiful blue shores.

The Troll always guards a bridge or gate. Pay the toll to enter his pine gates. He smiles at you, and what he can gaze upon.

The bravery of the Colonists created our nation. Their history belongs to us, and we must preserve and pass it on to future generations.

The purpose of my books is to educate and pass on a love of US history to others. Please help me share these adventures through your contacts and social media.

I would love to visit your communities for chats and book signings. Maybe you can invite me and teach me about your town's history?

My book's mapmakers did wonderful work. They asked if I would leave an X on the maps to mark where the Pirate left treasure. I said if they find the Pirate's mark, they would be pleased.

Unless you are wise, Lady Liberty's treasure lies forever under peaceful, starry skies. You must be persistent, have hope, and all will go well.

This work covers the Northeast States, similar to Forrest Fenn's *The Thrill of the Chase* in New Mexico, Colorado, Wyoming, Yellowstone National Park, and Montana. Forrest hid one chest; Lady Liberty may have hid many more to spread out the love for intrepid treasure hunters. The population in the Northeast is much larger. It made sense to create more opportunities for folks to enjoy traveling with loved ones while seeking the glory of finding some treasure with their family and friends.

College students may wish to form treasure-hunting clubs to compete against other rival schools to see who is the best on this treasure-hunting quest.

Have safe fun *Remembering America* as you happily participate in *Lady Liberty's Treasure Hunt* or *Riley's Treasure Chase*. *Lady Liberty's Treasure* awaits you beneath starry skies. Turn on the great songs "Heartbeat" by Red 7 and "Red Skies" by The Fixx then embark on your quest.

In the years ahead, please play "America" by Simon & Garfunkle to remember me; and your great journey coming, and going across this section of America.

I randomly placed valuables and collectibles in *Lady Liberty's Treasure* and *Riley's Treasure*. The adult treasure hunt is more difficult to find so that prize is more valuable than the children's treasure. As I typed these words "Peace Train" by Cat Stevens, "Kind and Generous" by Natalie Merchant, and "Blackbird" by the Beatles were softly playing in background. Their music brings me back to quieter times.

The below listed items; that I collected over my lifetime; are worth over $100,000 US dollars in 2024, and are physically out there in treasure chests for someone to locate them in the years ahead:

British Silver The Royal Celebration 10 OZ. .999 Silver Bars

Archangel Michael 10 OZ .999 Silver Bars

Rare 1947 Seal 50 Cent piece

(2) France Napoleon 1 rare 1 Decime 1814

France Napoleon 1813 Silver Coin

France 1580 Henry III Double Sol Parisis Silver

English King Henry III Medieval 1216 – 1272 A.D.

(2) Medieval England Henry VIII First Coinage

US 1910 Gold $10 Indian Head Eagle

US 1908 Gold $10 Indian Head Eagle

US Gold $5 Indian head

US Gold $2.5 Indian Head

France 1583 Silver Double Sol Parisis Henry III

France 2020 Silver $10 Euro Lafayette to Boston

Colonial Spanish 1400's Silver Cob Pirate Coins

Colonial Spanish 1600's Pirate Shipwreck Cob Coins

Spanish 1869 – 1890 5 Cent pieces

Spanish Mid 1840's – 1860 coins

Spanish 1820 – 1840 Maravedis coins

Spanish 1800 – 1820 Maravedis coins

Spanish 1700 – 1799 Maravedis coins

Spanish 1600's Pirate Cobs

Spanish Shipwreck 1826 Pirate Coin Real

Numerous US Buffalo Head Nickels

Numerous US Silver Peace Dollars

Numerous US Silver Morgan Dollars

US Eisenhower Bicentennial Silver dollars

1976 US Kennedy Half Dollars

US 1975 - 1976 Bicentennial Quarters

Irish Connemara Marble Jewelry

1700's Colonial Powder Horns

1885 Stanley London reproduction compass

Old style reproduction telescope

Original US Civil War Era Cavalry or Officers Telescope

Several Forrest Fenn *The Thrill of the Chase* treasure chest treasure coins

Several Forrest Fenn *The Thrill of the Chase* treasure relic pieces

US Grant Bronze Medals (US copies of 1863 original bronze medals)

1826 Spanish Colonial Shipwreck Pirate coin

1788 Spanish Colonial Pirate Shipwreck Coin

1808 Spanish Pirate Shipwreck Coin

1746 Spanish Pirate Coin

1825 Spanish Pirate Coin

Sterling Silver Bunker & Breeds Hill Boston Spoon

Sterling Silver Old North Church Boston Spoon

Rare 1825 Spanish Pirate Coin

Multiple 1870 Spanish Colonial Shipwreck Coins

1798 Spanish Colonial Shipwreck Pirate Coin

1600's Spanish Pirate Cob Coin

1987 France Lafayette Silver Coin

2020 France Euro Lafayette Silver 2 OZ. Coin

1847 Spanish Pirate Coin

1861 Spanish 1861 Pirate Coin

1840 Spanish Pirate Shipwreck Coins

Rare Roman Trajan Decius Silver Antoninus Coin

Rare Roman Empire Augustus Spanish Mint LLerda Coin

1802 Spanish ½ Reale Pirate Golden Era Coin

1778 Spanish Colonial ½ Reale Golden Era Pirate Coin

Rare 1700's Crusaders Spanish ½ Reale Segovia Coin

Rare 12th Century Crusaders Spanish ½ Reale Coin

Rare 1200's Medieval Spanish Coin

Rare 1600's Spanish Colonial Coin

1829 Spanish Shipwreck Pirate Coin

1868 Spanish Shipwreck Pirate Coin

1775 Spanish ½ Reale Charles III Colonial Coin

Pre Columbian Frog Style Jewelry Modern Pieces

Many NGC Rare & Precious Coin Slabs

1857 US $1 Gold Coins

1900 US Lafayette Commemorative Silver Dollars

US President Franklin Pierce (NH) Gold Coin

Rare Forrest Fenn *The Thrill of the Chase* Treasure Gold pieces

1775 Ireland/British Half Penny

1778 France Louis XVI Era Coins

1775 British King George III Half Penny

1775 British King George III North Wales Coin

Multiple 1775 – 1776 Hibernia Ireland British Half Pennies

Multiple 1775 English King George III Farthing Coins

Multiple Atocha Silver Pieces

Multiple Paul Revere's Ride ½ Troy OZ Silver Rounds

US Mint Medal General Nathaniel Greene

Stainless Steal Pirates Cross & Bones Necklaces

Paul Revere's Ride Medals

Battle of Concord Bronze Medals

1925 Lexington-Concord Sesquicentennial Silver Half Dollars

Bicentennial Paul Revere Medals

1925 US Commemorative Half Dollar

1976 Minuteman Monument Bronze Medal

2021 US General Washington Battle of Trenton Coins

Carlisle Minutemen Route to Concord Bronze Medal

.999 Silver Birth of the Nation Lexington & Concord Rounds

Battle of Lexington and Concord Medals

Bicentennial Warning Riders Token Medal

Lexington & Concord Bicentennial Token Medals

Lexington "What a Glorious Morning" Medal

1930's Black Ruthenium 24K Buffalo Coins

US Gold Plated Buffalo Nickels

1976 Gold Plated JFK Half Dollars

US 1965 Silver Half Dollars (in honor of Laurel's year of birth)

US 1963 Silver Franklin Half dollars (in honor of the Author's birth year)

1946 Silver Walking Half Dollar

1976 US Mint Proof Coin Sets

1976 Philadelphia Bicentennial Quarters

1976 General Stark Bicentennial Bronze Medals

US Civil War Medals & Civil War Era Powder Flasks

US Civil War Artist Don Troiani Cased Coin

1812 US Bust Half Dollars

1812 France Napoleon .90 Silver Coin

American Revolution US or British Dropped Bullet & US Civil War Relic Bullets

State of Liberty Centennial .925 Sterling Silver Token

Extremely Important Historical Figures rare written words with baseball card COA's

Various Rare Historic Tokens, Medals, Coins and Other Collectibles

Extremely Valuable .925 Sterling Silver 15 Oz Pirate Skull Statue Artwork

Rare Forrest Fenn style Wyoming Jade "Slick" Necklace to bring you good luck

US .999 Pure Silver Buffalo Silver Round

Extremely Rare "Fairmont Collection" US $5 Gold Liberty Coins

Undisclosed amount Finder's Reward, if you carefully follow the written instructions in the chest after finding a *Lady Liberty's Treasure Hunt* or *Riley's Treasure Chase* treasure.

FURTHER READING:

The Thrill of the Chase by Forrest Fenn (his treasure chest was found)

Eric Sloane's America by Eric Sloane

Lafayette in America by Louis Gottschalk

Toward Lexington by by John Shy

American Barns and Covered Bridges by Eric Sloane

Rise to Rebellion by Jeffrey Shaara

The Spirits of '76 by Eric Sloane

The Road to Taos by Eric Sloane

Ethan Allen by John Pell

A. Lassell Ripley Paintings by Edward Weeks

The Legend of Sleepy Hollow by Washington Irving

Washington's Crossing by David Hackett Fischer

In the Hands of Providence by Alice Rains Trulock

John Paul Jones by Evan Thomas

One Continuous Fight by Eric Whittenberg

Paul Revere's Ride by David Hackett Fischer

Trenton and Princeton 1776 - 1777 by David Bonk

The Secret by Byron Preiss (some of his treasures are still out there)

In Search of Liberty by James Bell

The Minutemen by John R. Galvin

The Battle of April 19, 1775 by Frank Warren Coburn

Paul Revere's Ride by Henry W. Longfellow; Illustrated by Monica Vachula

Return to Taos by Eric Sloane

The Landing by Rochambeau by Michael Davidson

Henry Knox: Visionary General of the American Revolution by Mark Pulls

Light-Horse Harry by Noel Gerson

Morristown: a Military Capital of the American Revolution by Melvin Weig

The Revolutionary War in Bennington County by Richard Smith

The Battle for New York by Barnet Schecter

Don Troiani's Soldiers of the American Revolution by Don Troiani and James Kochan

Don Troiani's Campaign Saratoga 1777 by Don Troiani and Eric Schnitzer

Don Troiani's Black Soldiers in American Wars by John Rees

One Gallant Rush by Peter Burchard

They Met at Gettysburg by Edward Stockpole

The Passing of Armies by Joshua Brewer Chamberlain

The St. Albans Raid by Michelle Sherburne

A Vermont Cavalry Man in War & Love Edited by Elliott Hoffman

The First Vermont Cavalry in the Civil War by Joseph Collea

Toward Gettysburg A Biography of General John Reynolds by E.J. Nichols

The Irish at Gettysburg by Phillip Tucker

The Killer Angels by Michael Shaara (Easton Press: Illustrated by Mort Kunstler)

From Manassas to Appomattox by General James Longstreet

Riley's Treasure Chase (young adult reader) by Michael Cloherty O'Connell

ADAMS SCHOOL
1972-73
MRS. CLINTON   GRADE 4
MR. JACOBUS-PRIN.

"We all loved Mrs. Clinton!" (Adams School class photo)

Riley' Treasure Chase is a companion book for children, their families & friends

"The two most important days of your life; are the day you were born,
and the day you find out why (Mark Twain)."
Remember the past; live in the present, and dream of tomorrow.
May your efforts, and intuition serve you well. Godspeed.

Carpe Diem
MMXXV

ABOUT THE AUTHOR

American Revolutionary War and United States Civil War Historian Michael Cloherty O'Connell's career in public service spans more than four decades. He was born in Arlington; and grew up in Historic East Lexington near the First Blow for Liberty, and the Shot heard Round the World. He graduated from Lexington High School then earned a Bachelor's Degree at Northeastern University, Master's Degrees from Boston University, and Boston College. The author still lives in the Boston suburbs; with his beautiful wife Laurel, and is the proud father of four children. Michael has been actively involved in Scouting, coaching sports, and other positive youth activities all of his teenage, and adult life.